# Haiku – Ikebana

by Elena Malec

**March 2017**

# Ikebana as a holon

As a poet I enjoy meditation before I find inspiration to write. As an artist I enjoy shape, form, asymmetry in composition, color and light to create a painting. In my search for simplicity I discovered the haiku and zen philosophy. In my search for the essence of zen I discovered ikebana. Ikebana is the fusion between poetry and the visual arts. Ikebana is a number of stems, branches, so is the haiku, a number of syllables. Haiku is kigo and ikebana is seasonal, haiku is a part and the whole, so is ikebana a branch hinting for the tree. A haiku has the perfection of a mandala, and ikebana should have an imperfection, an asymmetry that does not allow to add anything to it because it reached its perfection. Being a branch and the tree, ikebana is a holon, a snowflake in haiku is the kigo word for winter.

Ikebana as a holon is part and whole, is imperfect and perfect at the same time. Ikebana is an esthetics of open forms in the realm of visual arts. The idea of open form is not new and maybe the best example of defining open form in art has been presented in Umberto Eco's work OPERA APERTA published in 1962. With reference to aesthetic works, Eco defines the open form internally dynamic and the fields of meaning open. Ikebana is Form as the meaning is open, left to the guessing and from this derives the esthetic pleasure of the viewer. Contours are diffuse, shapes and volumes suggested rather than imposed on the viewer, yet there is a place for order into chaos. On a philosophical level the art of ikebana is a response to an elusive reality, that escapes clear definition, has open answers and leaves room to imagination, dreaming, recreating meaning according to one's own abilities and needs for esthetic harmony.

The way the season can be read in the color of leaves makes ikebana's leaf a tree and a season, at another level a holon.

The haiku invites the visual to recreate an arrangement using minimalism, simplicity, wabi sabi, asymmetry.

> a single branch ikebana-
> shadows of furry catkins
> on a blank wall

alcove with hanging scroll-
fragrant honeysuckle
in reverence


The visual brings about its poetry. Holly (ilex canariensis) and chestnuts. Late autumn, winter time.

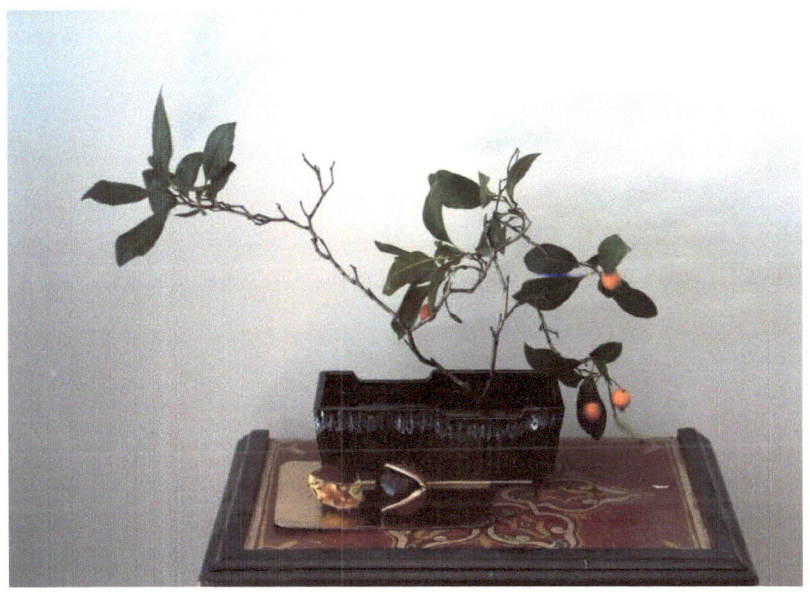

empty room-
vase with Indian hawthorn
in scalene triangle

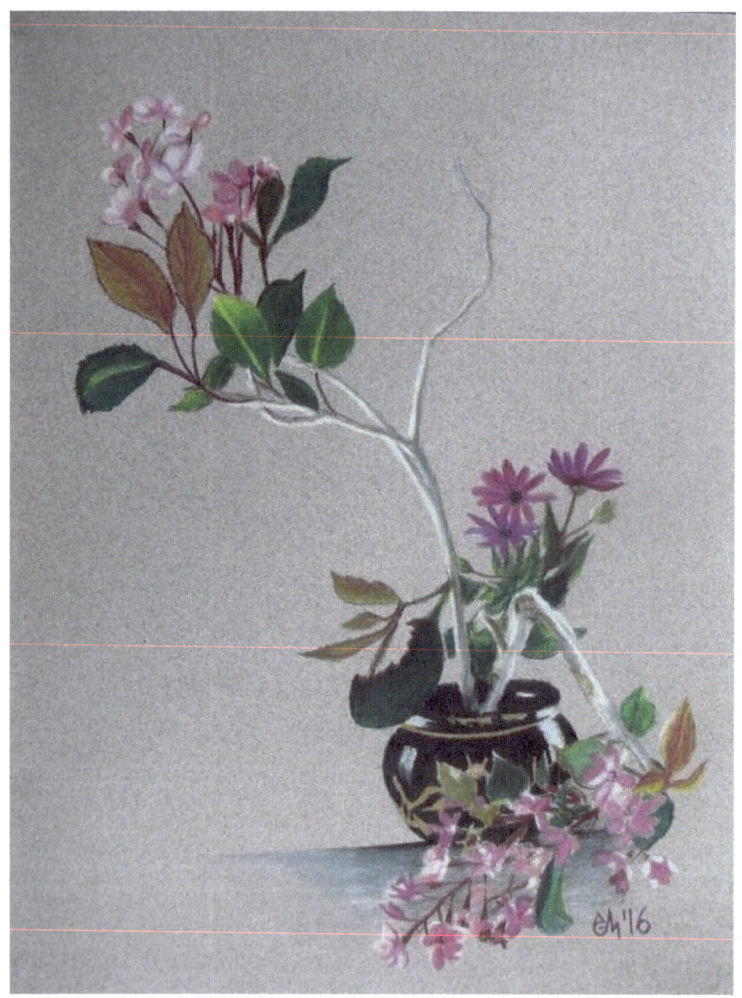

Elena Malec

Published in International Journal of Ikebana Studies, Vol.4, 2016

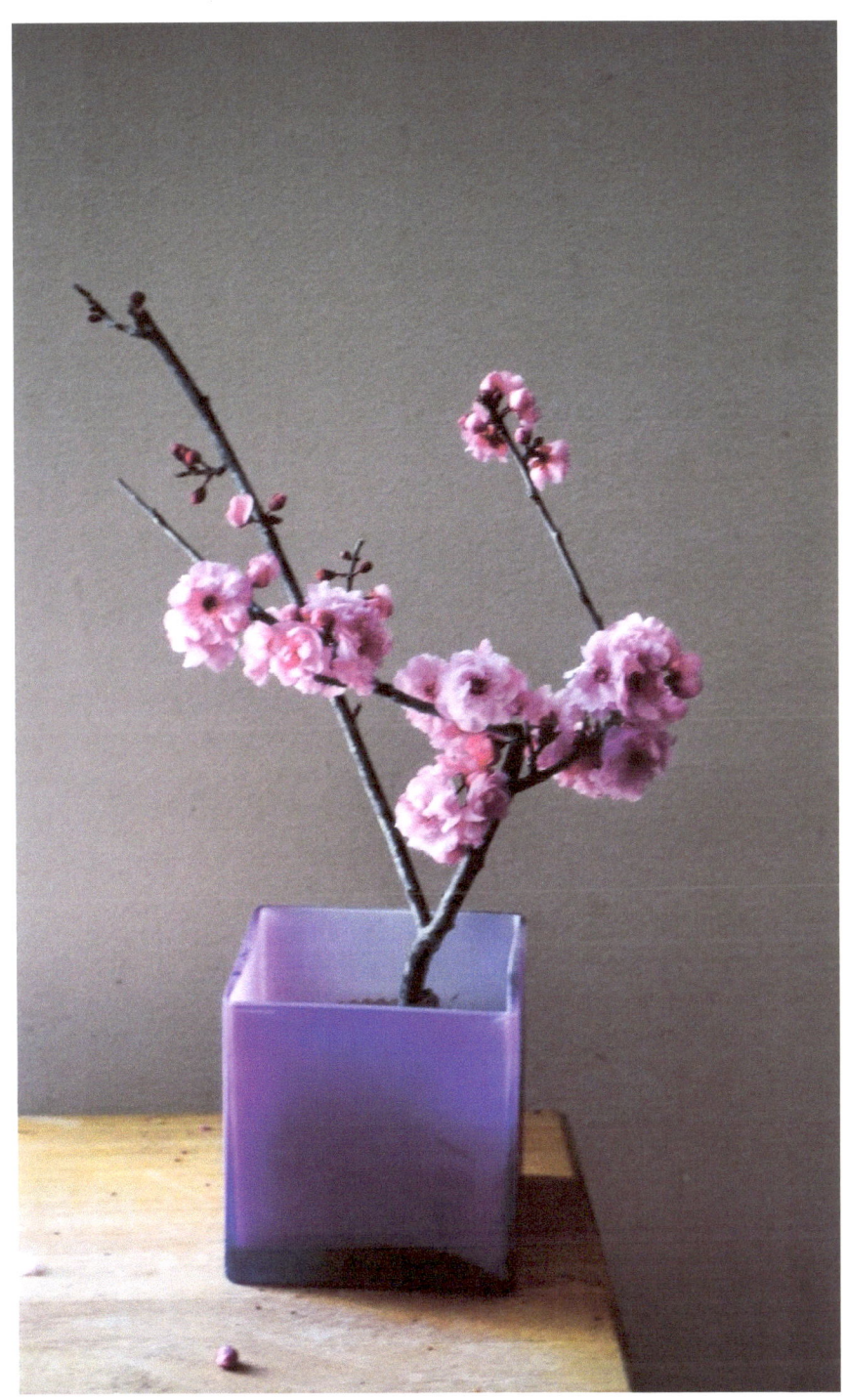

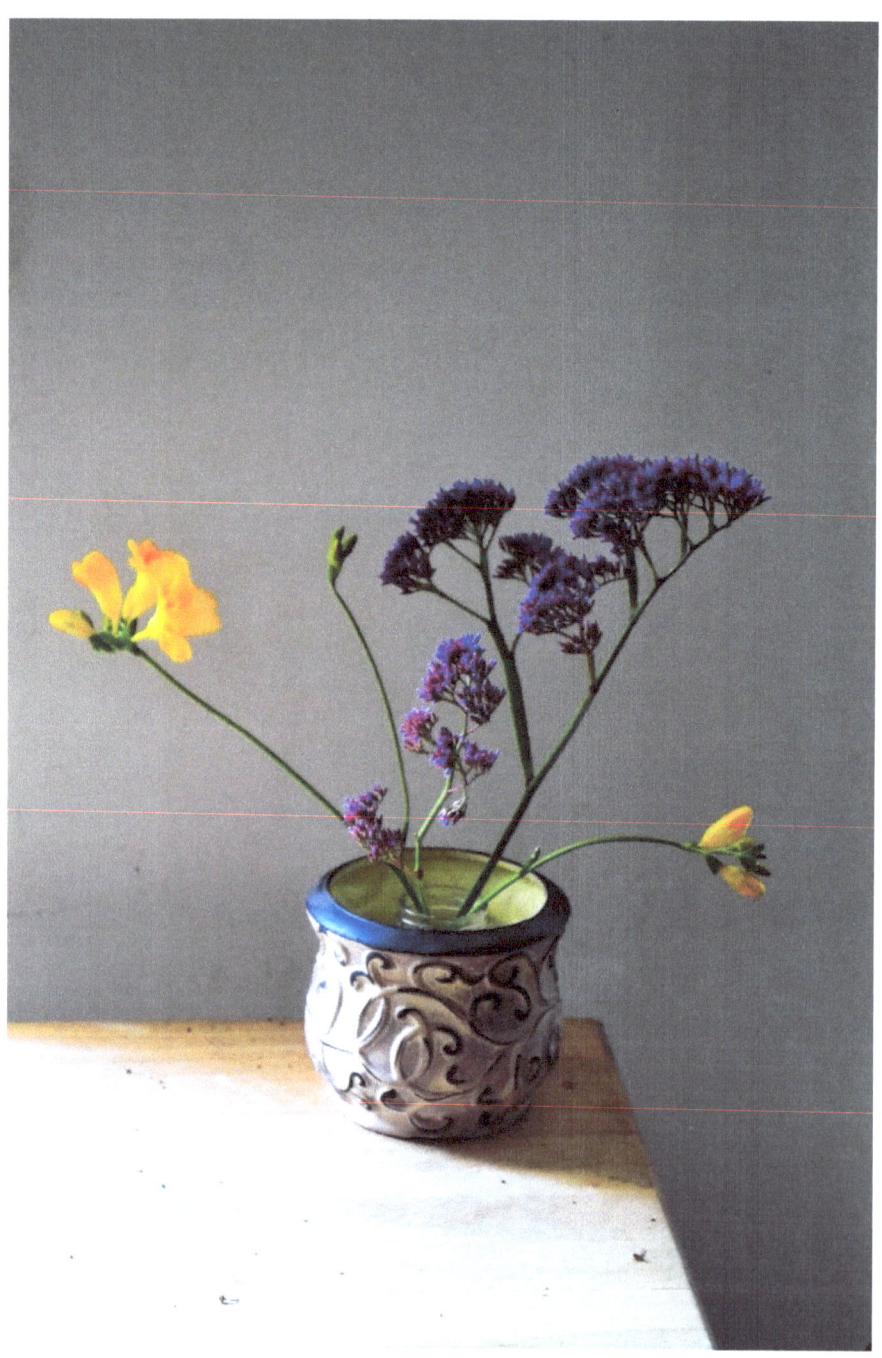

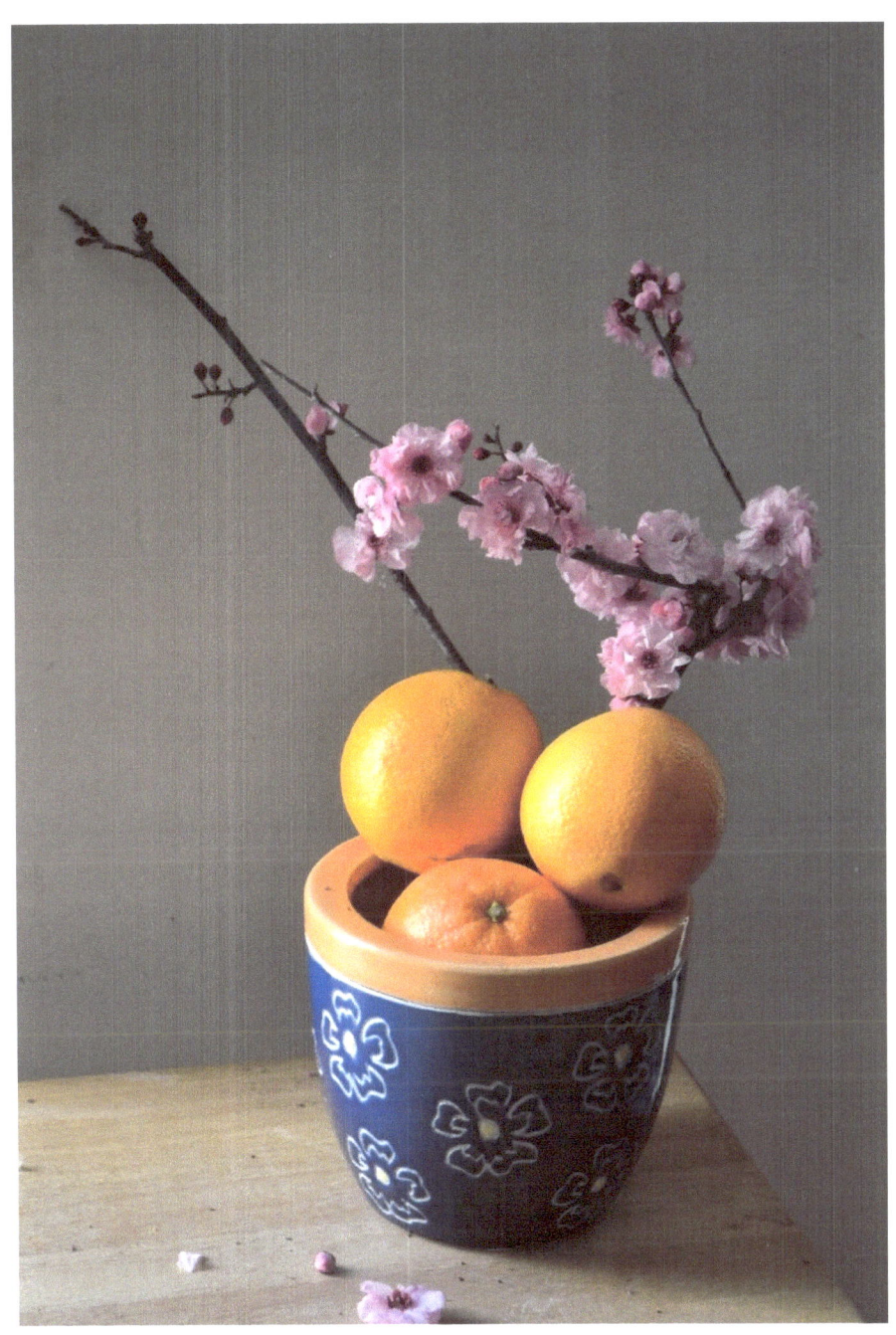

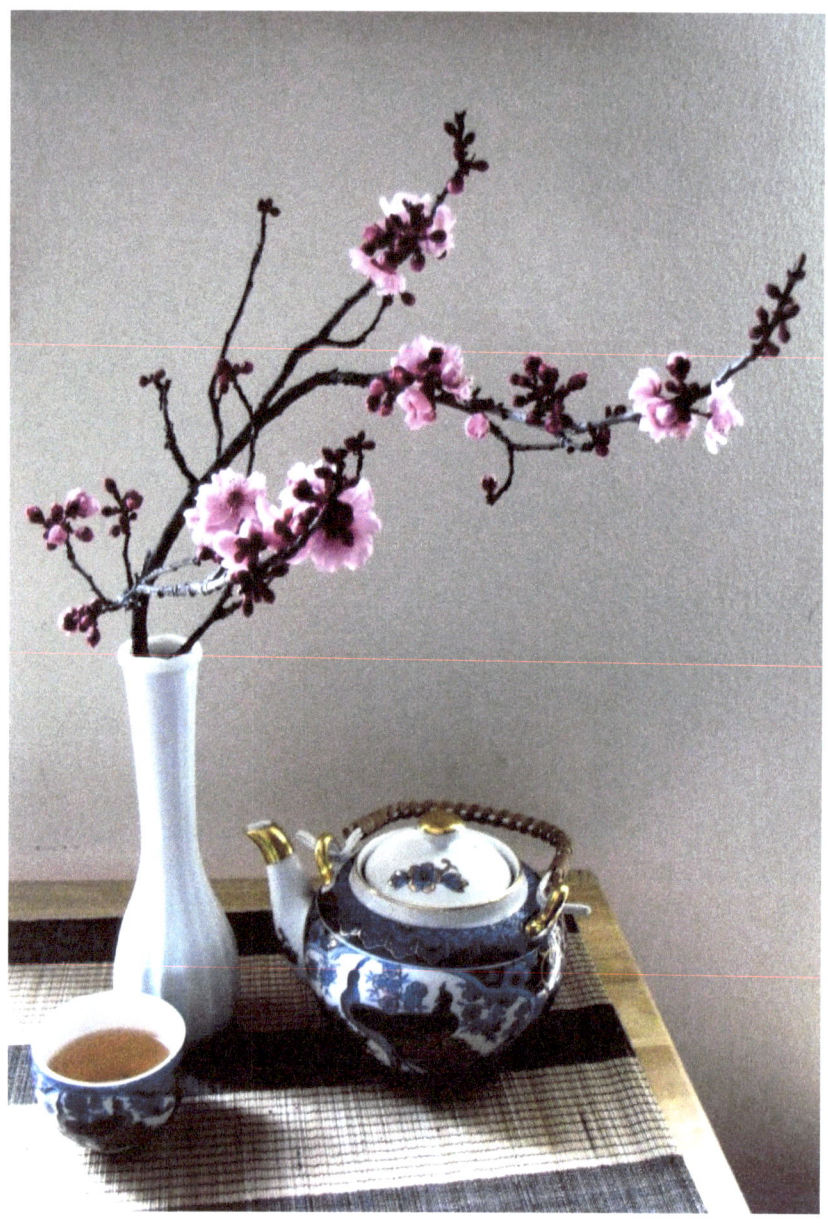

graceful maiko-
the ivory tea scoop
in gloved hands

morning chill-
China cup with steaming
chrysanthemum tea

tropical hillside-
women in colorful saris
picking the tea

yerba mate-
drinking with friends from
a hollow gourd

Grand bazaar-
the rug seller offers
hot apple tea

airline service-
tea from plastic carafe
no sugar tong

dog days-
supermarkets ran out
of iced tea

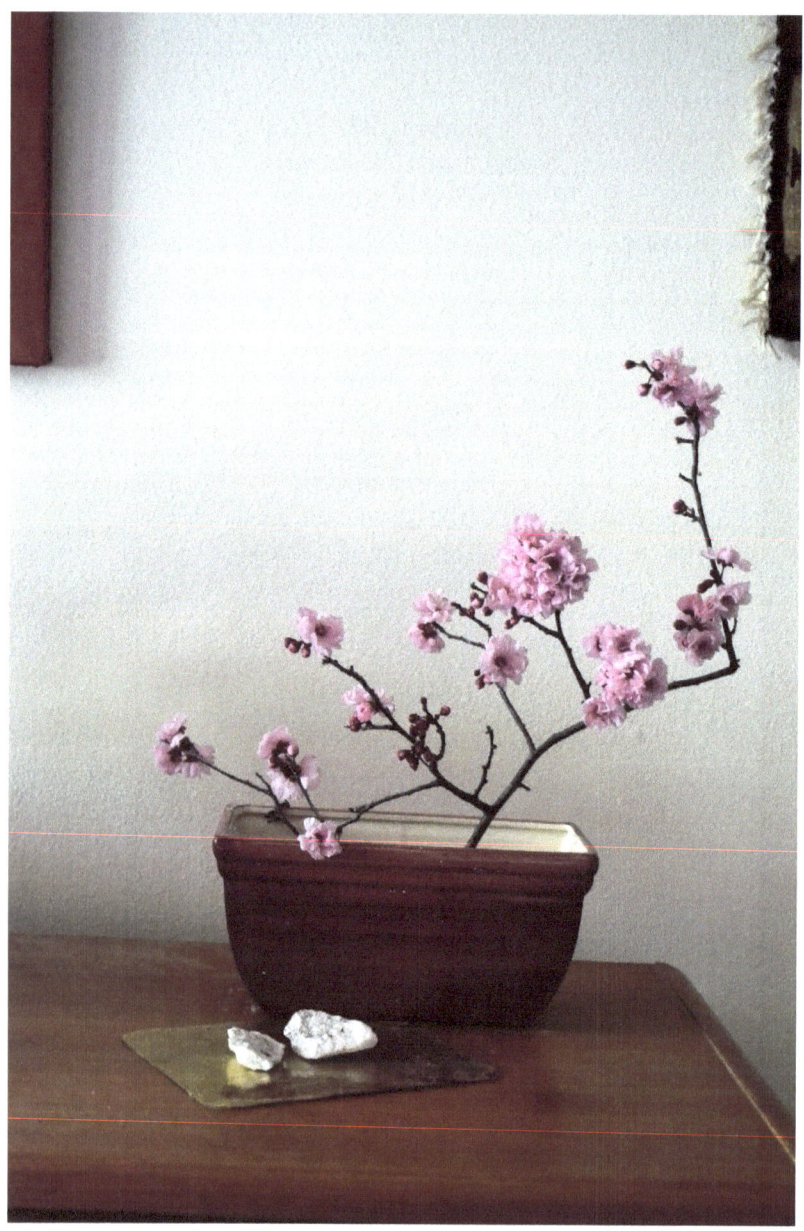

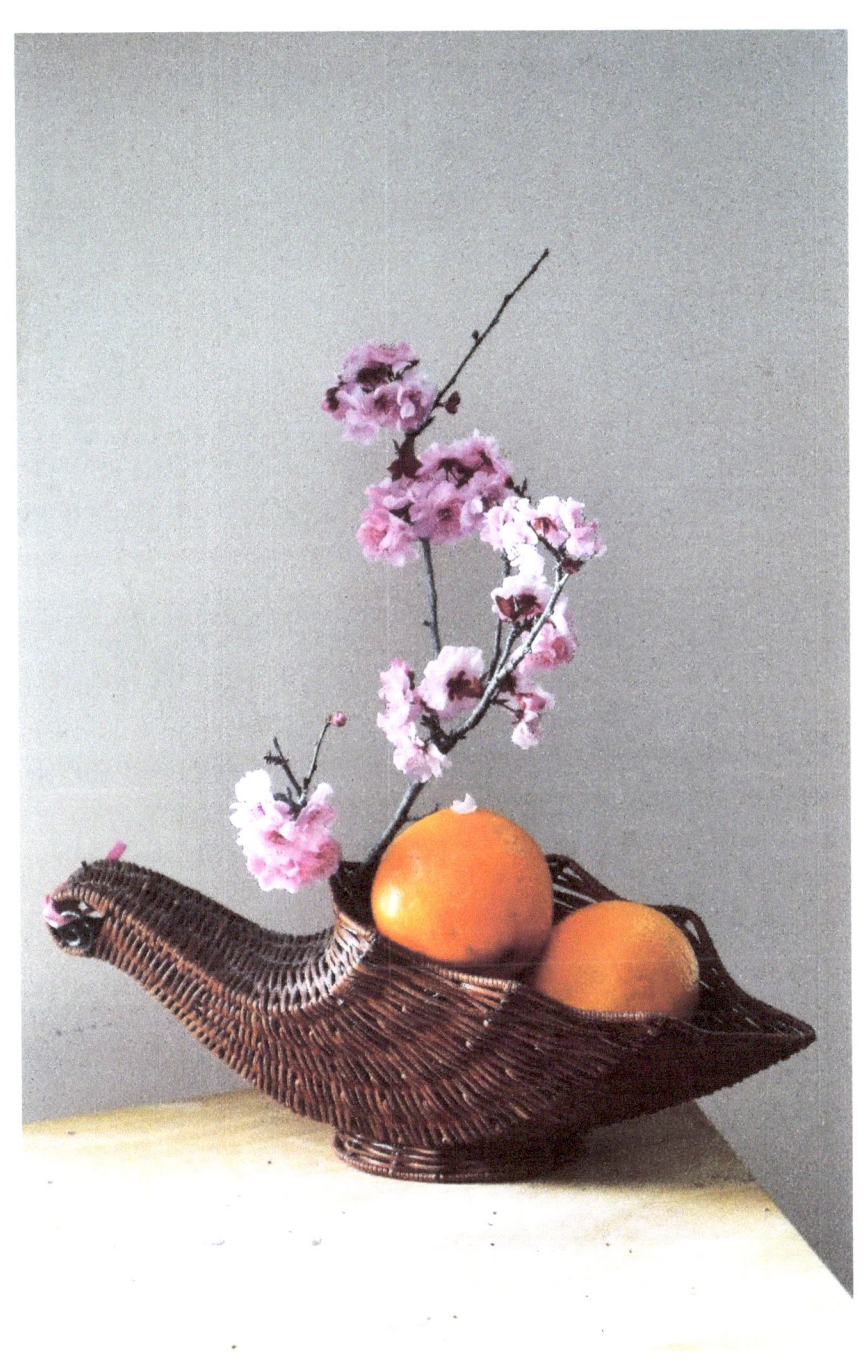

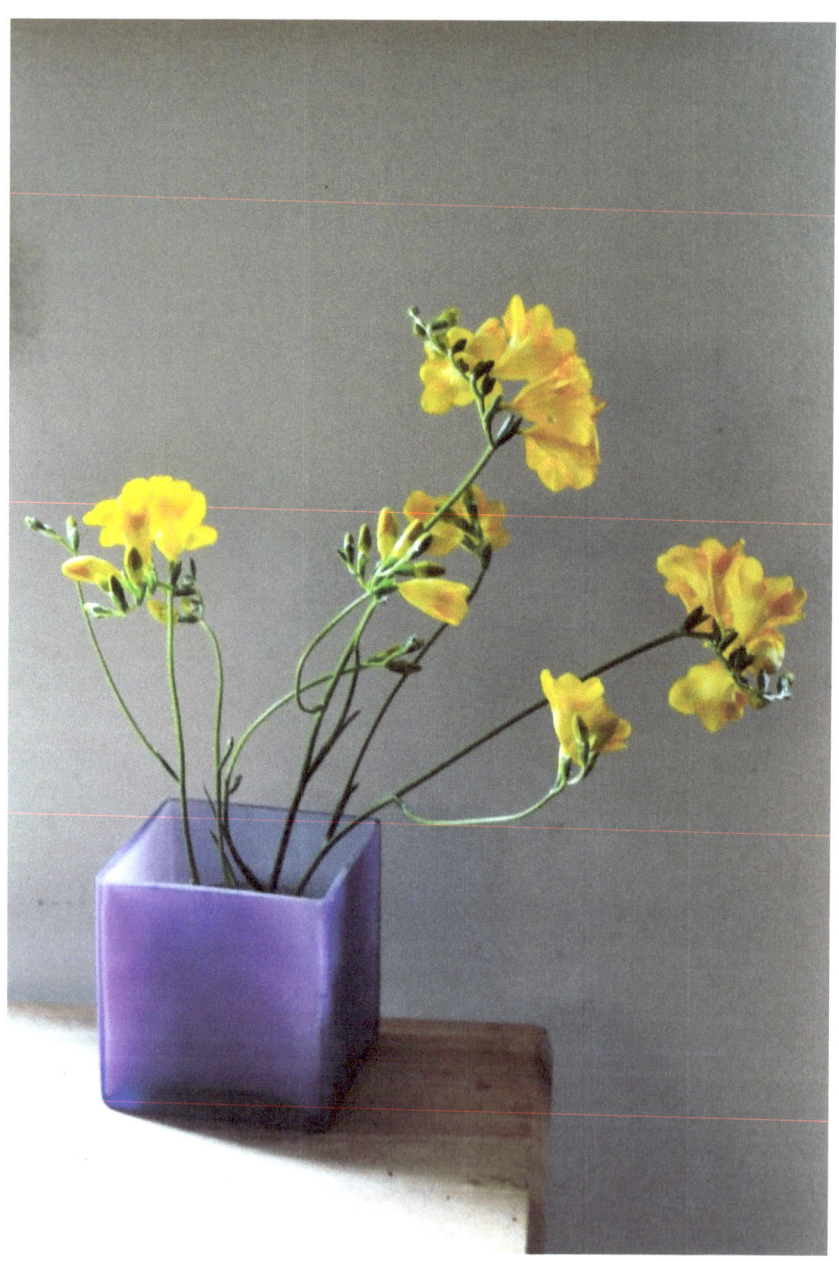

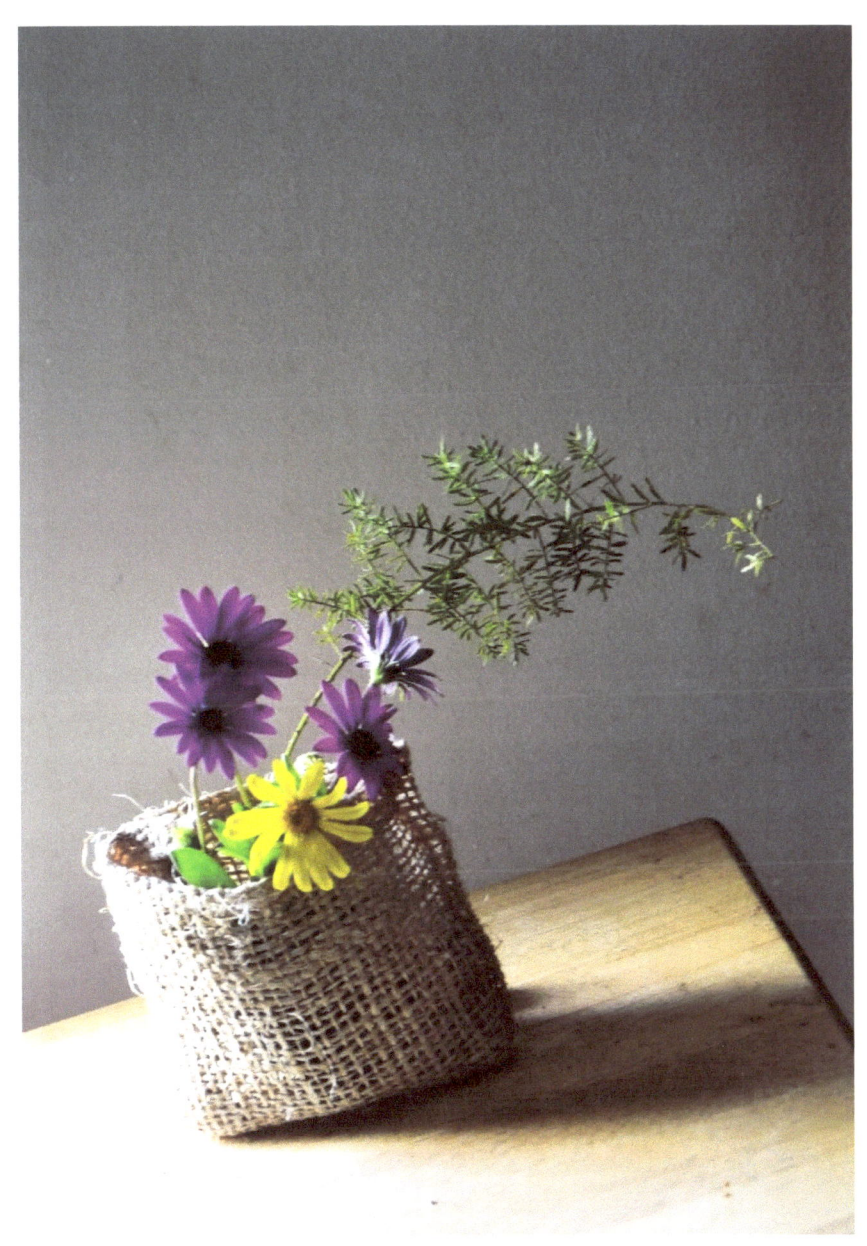

red onion in a basket-
between heaven and earth
green shoots


empty room-
vase with Indian hawthorn
in scalene triangle


kenzan and scissors-
the outdoor pine tree
missing a new shoot


shallow ceramic vase-
yellow buttons reflected
in the water


baby breath flower-
arrangement with gravel
all white

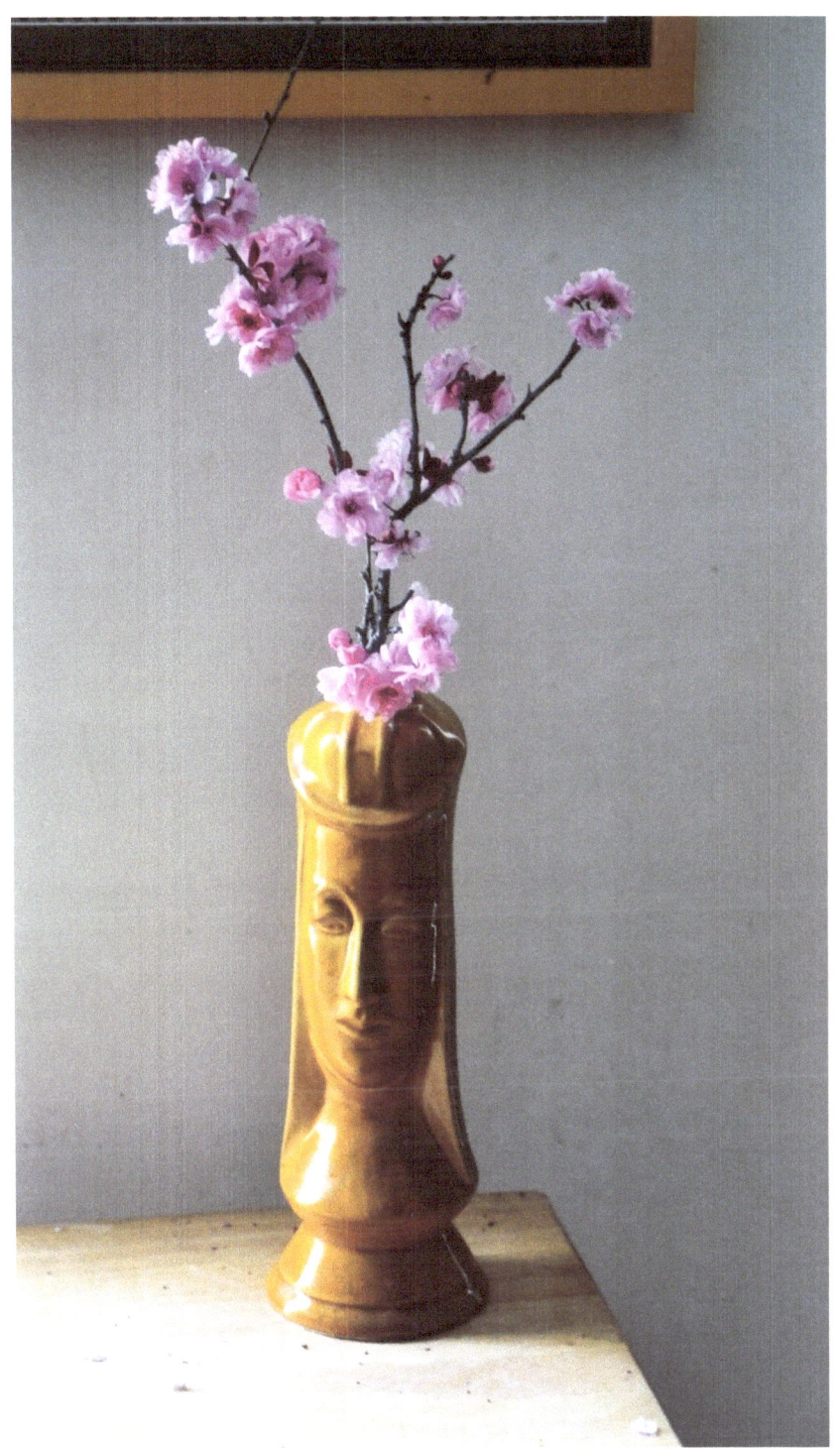

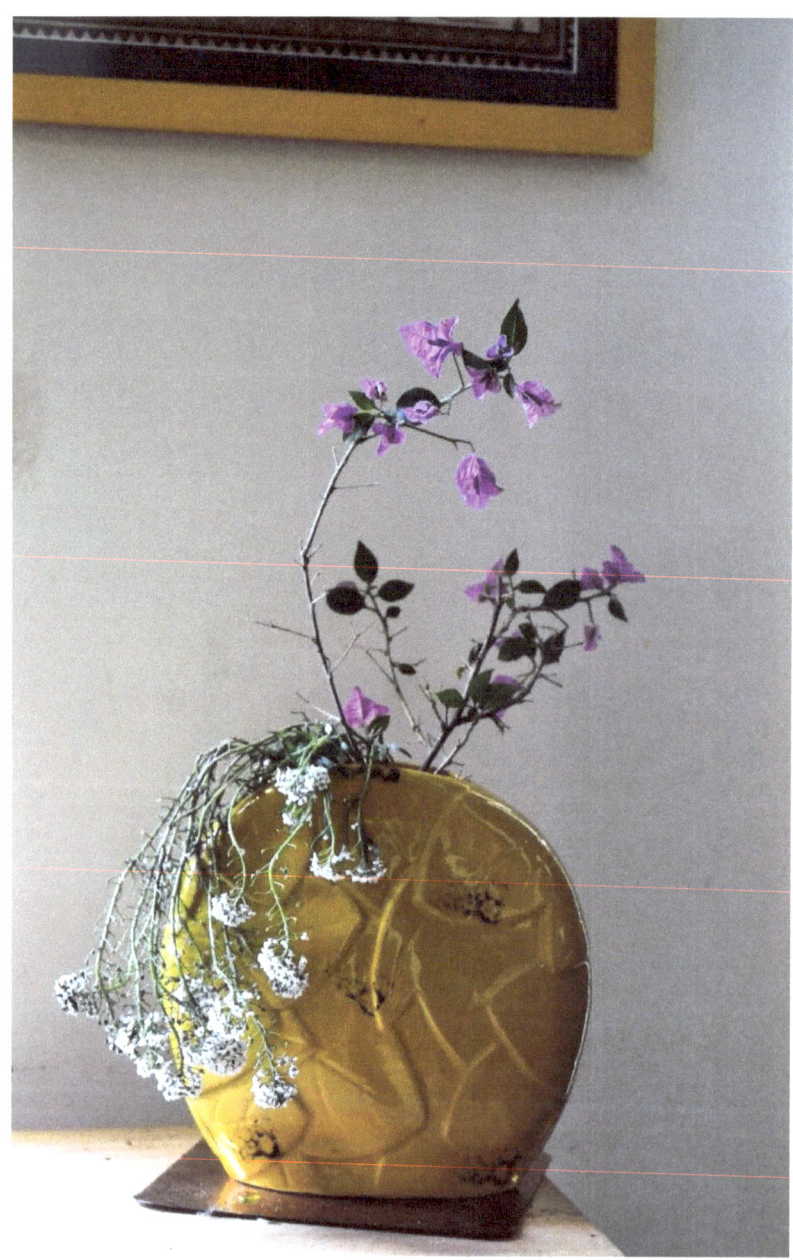

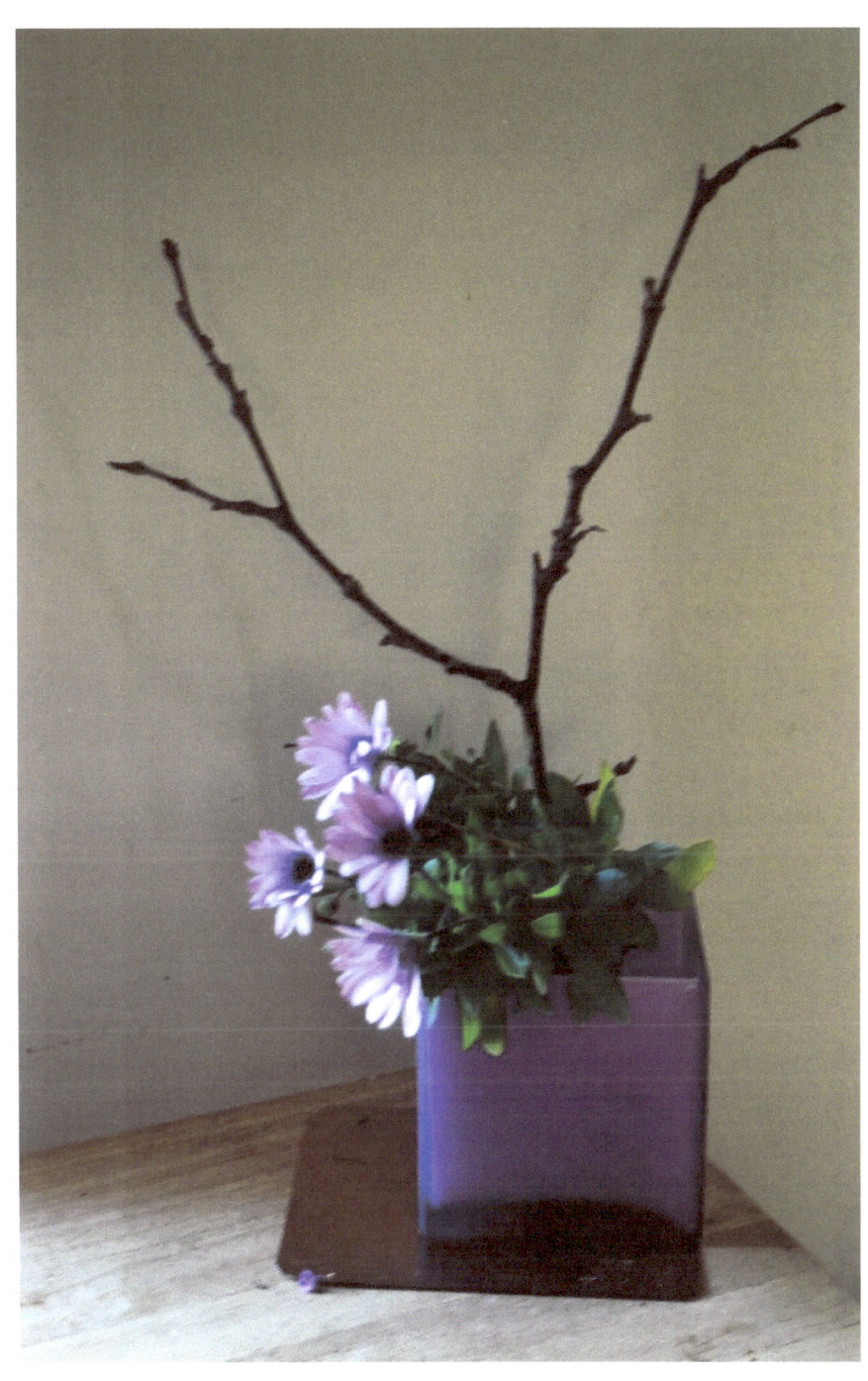

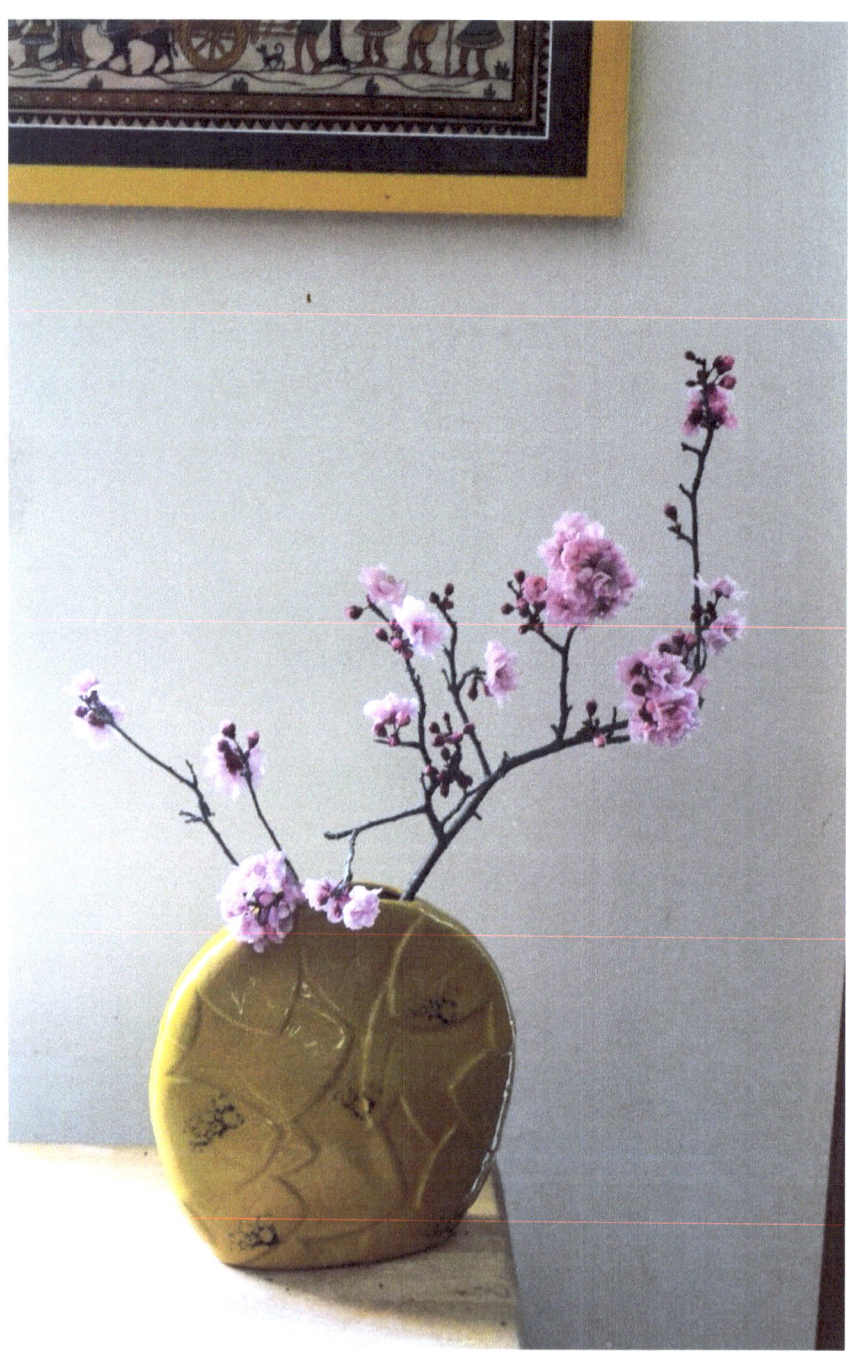

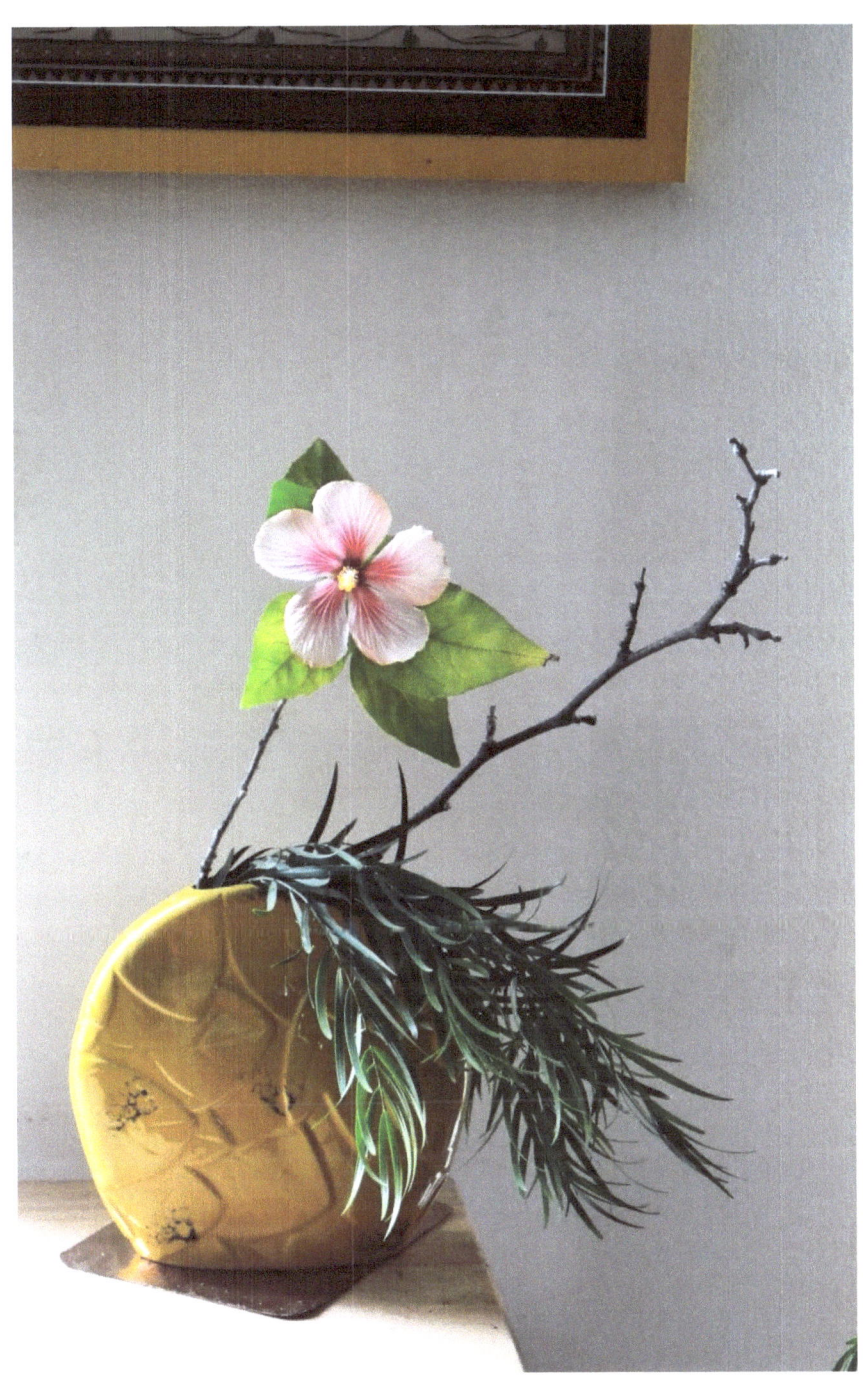

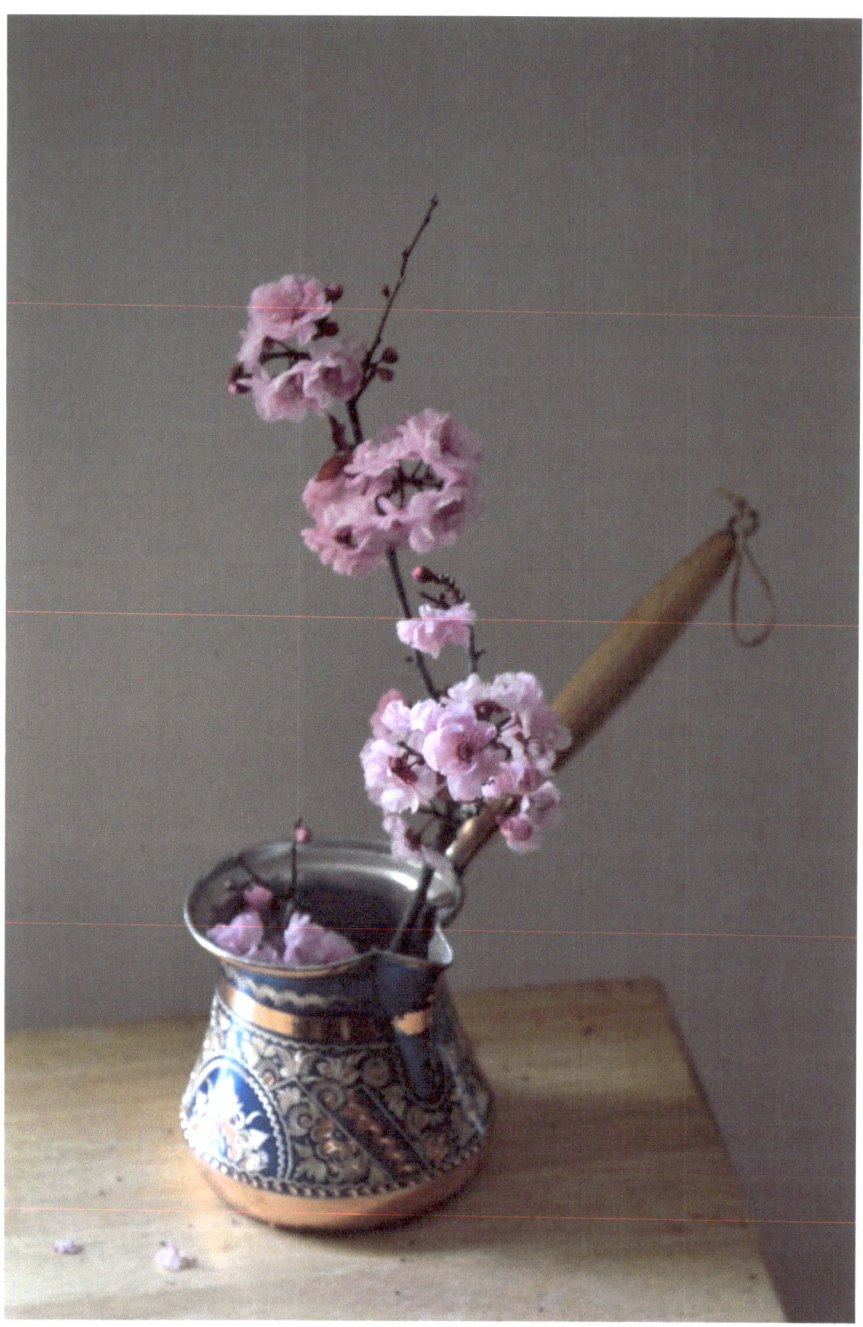

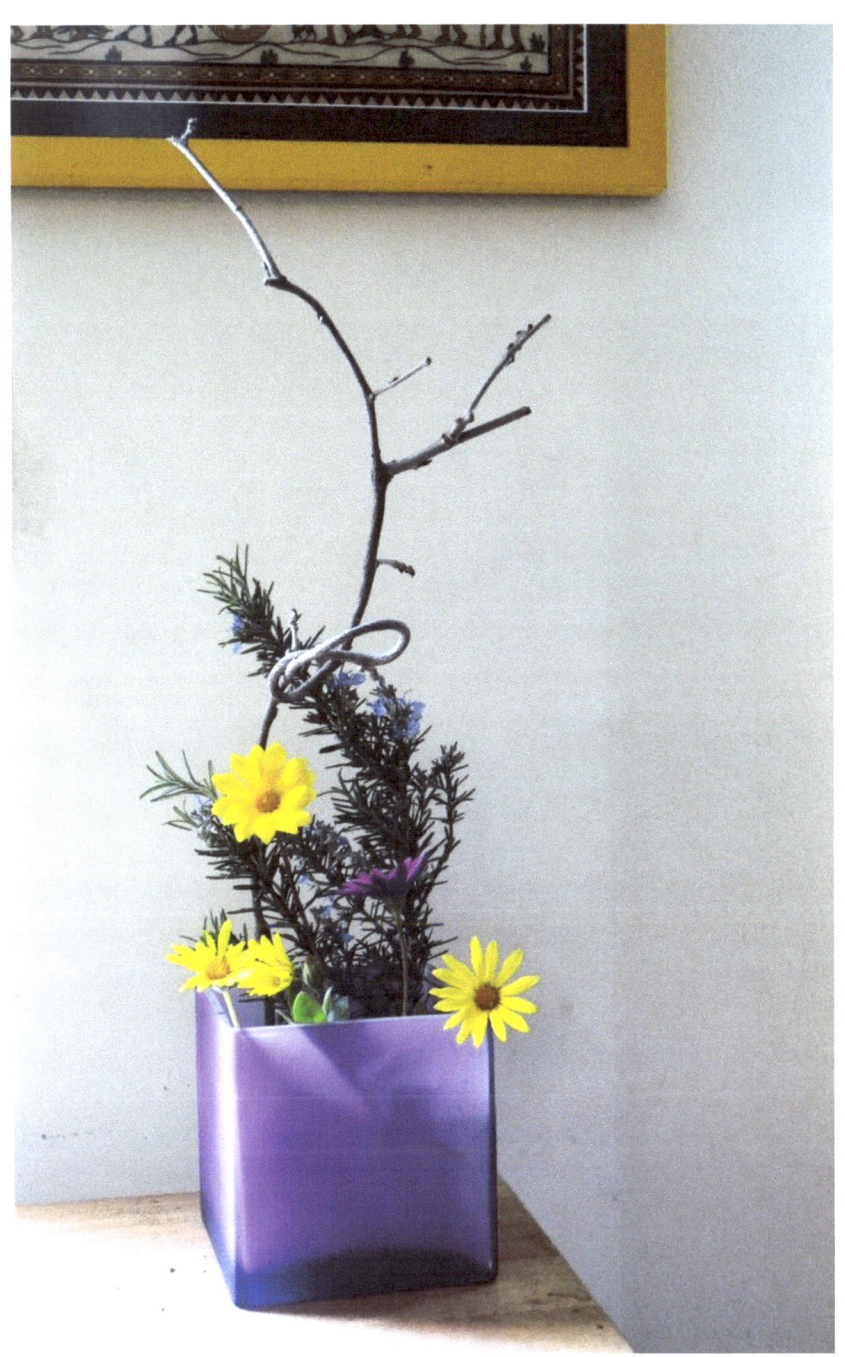

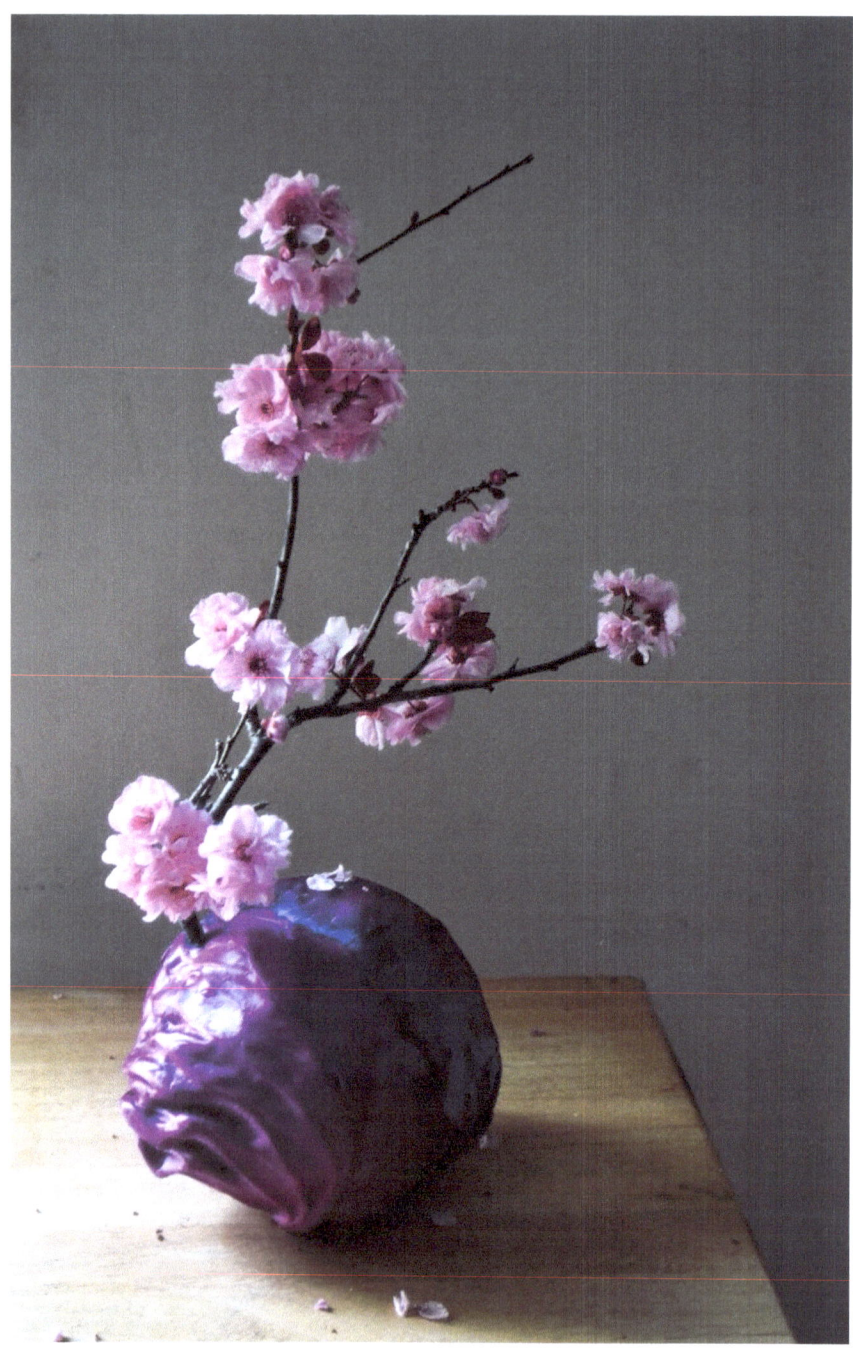

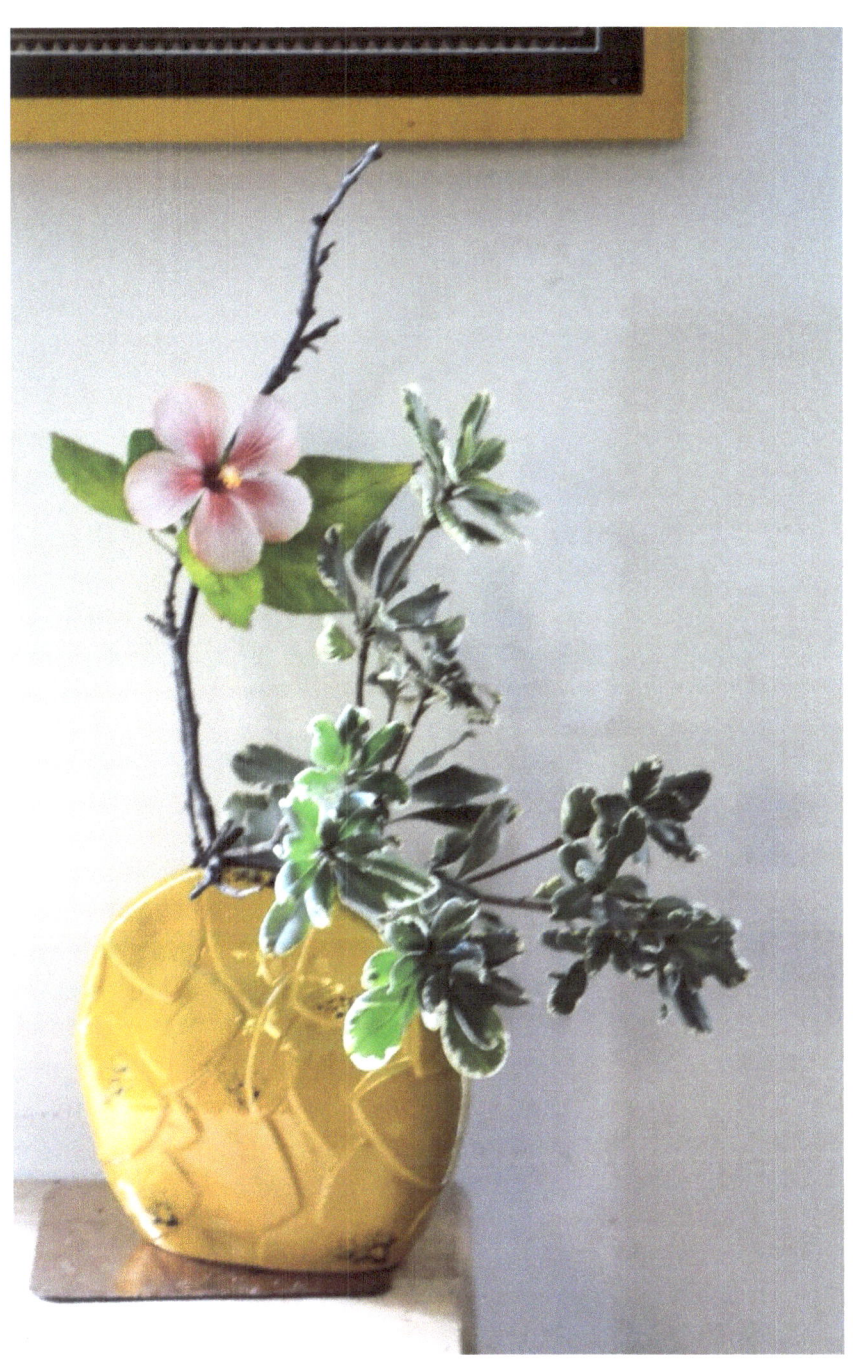

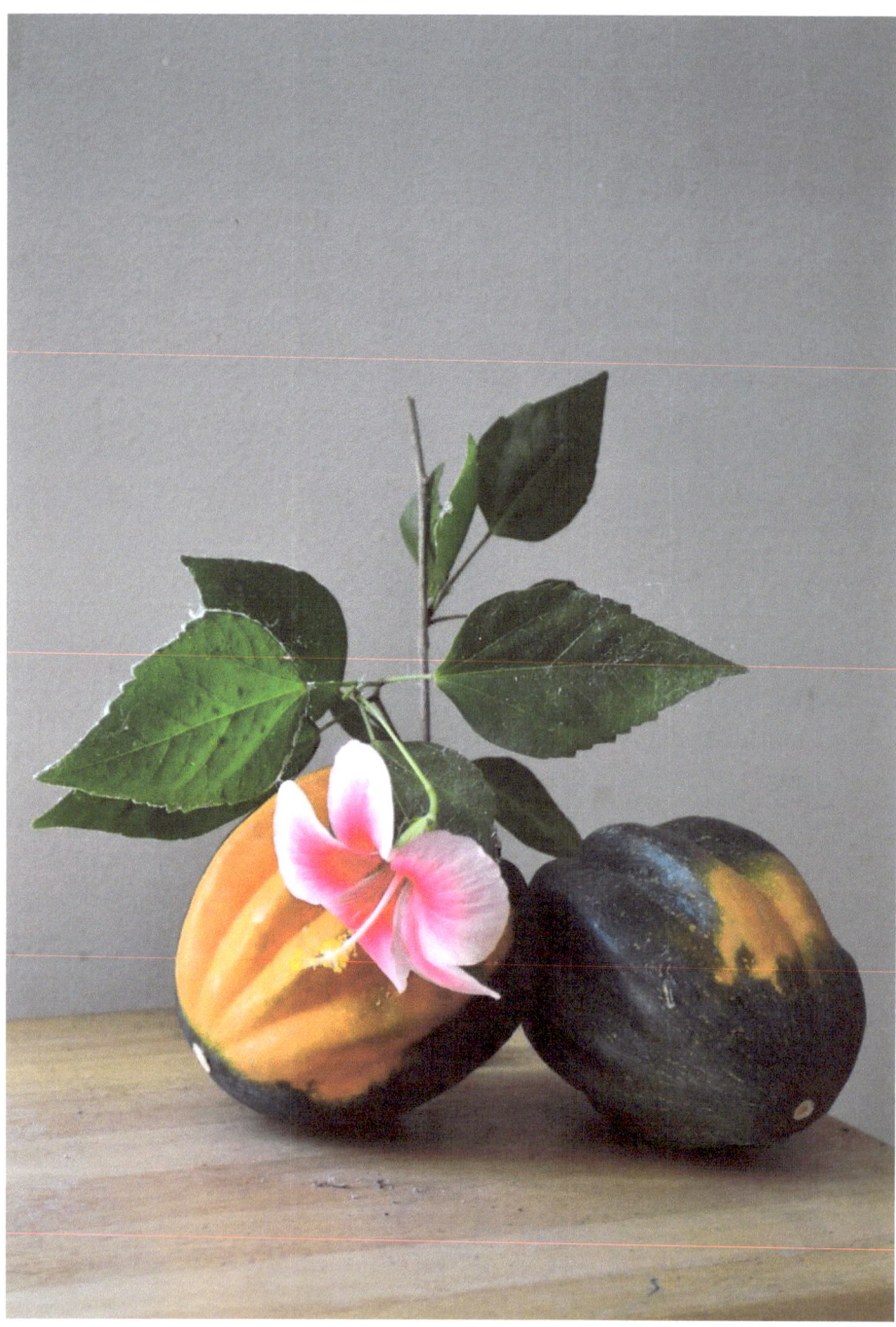

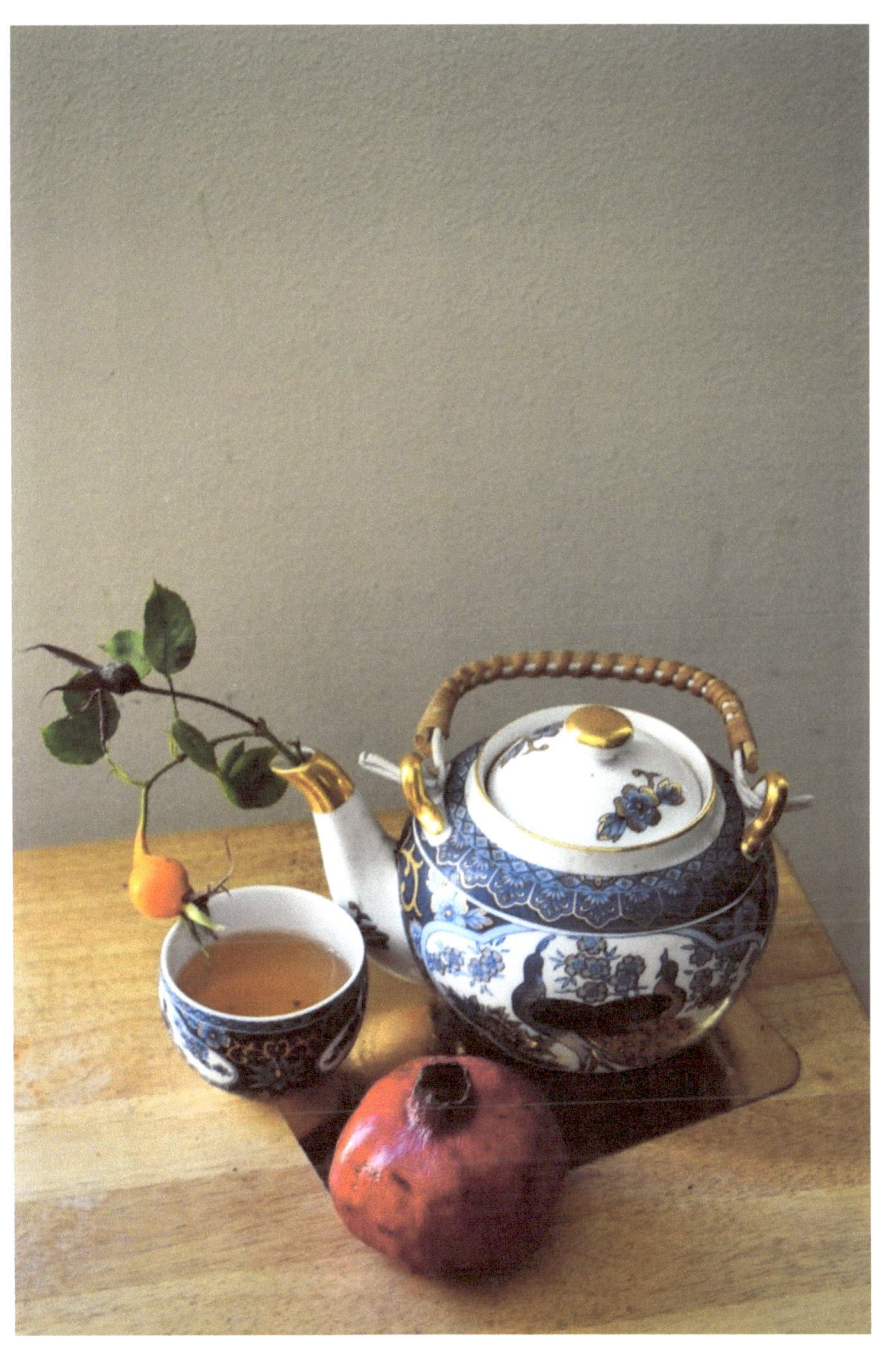

wild rose hips-
small ikebana in the spout
of a blue teapot

Siberian night-
using dry pinecones
for the samovar


desert moonlight-
camels and Bedouins around
the tea kettle


Tibetan monastery-
sipping butter tea from
wooden bowls

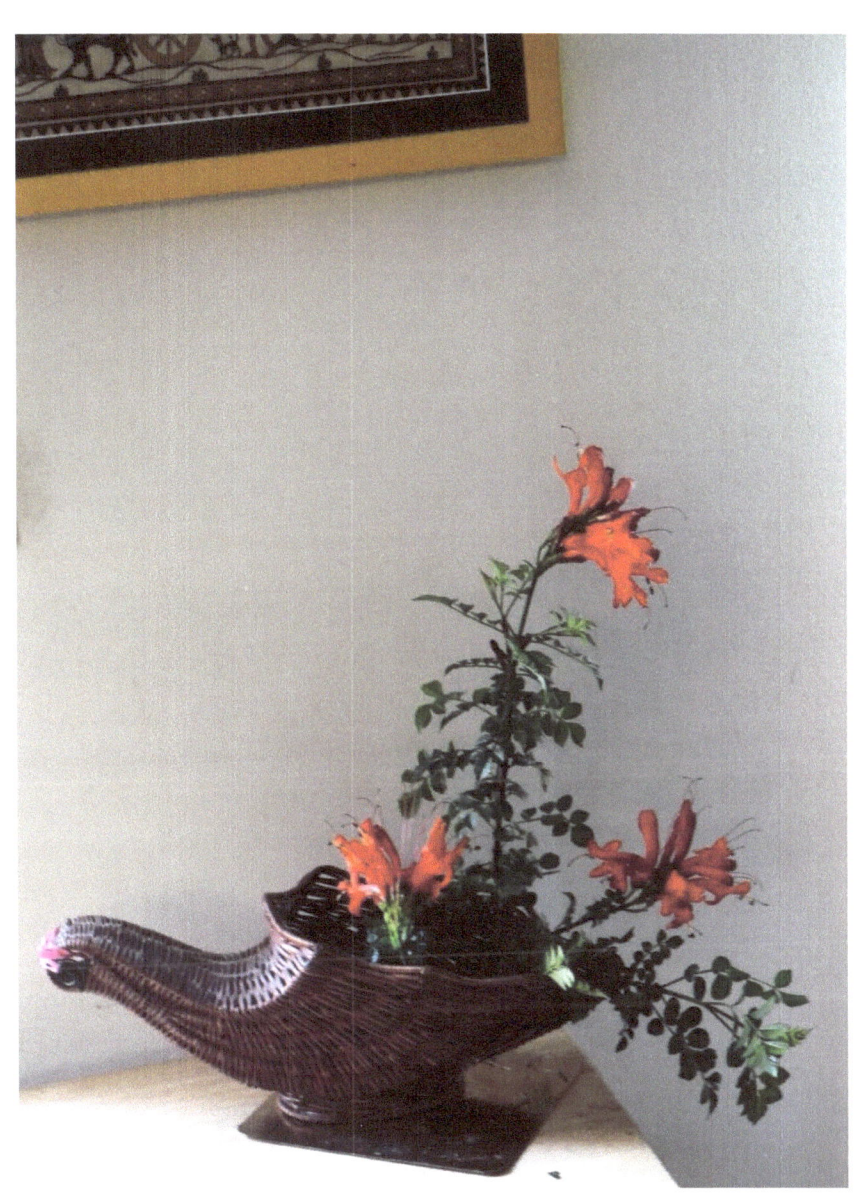

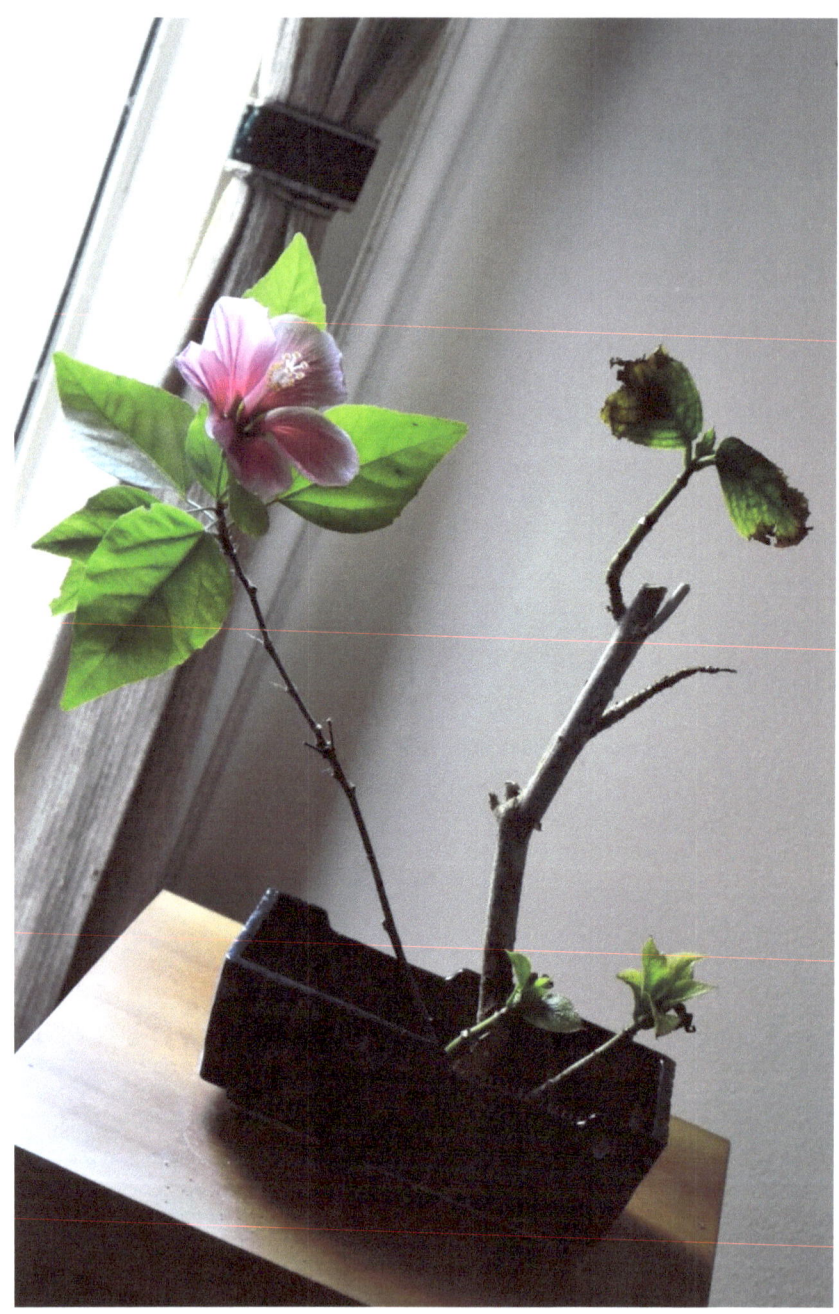

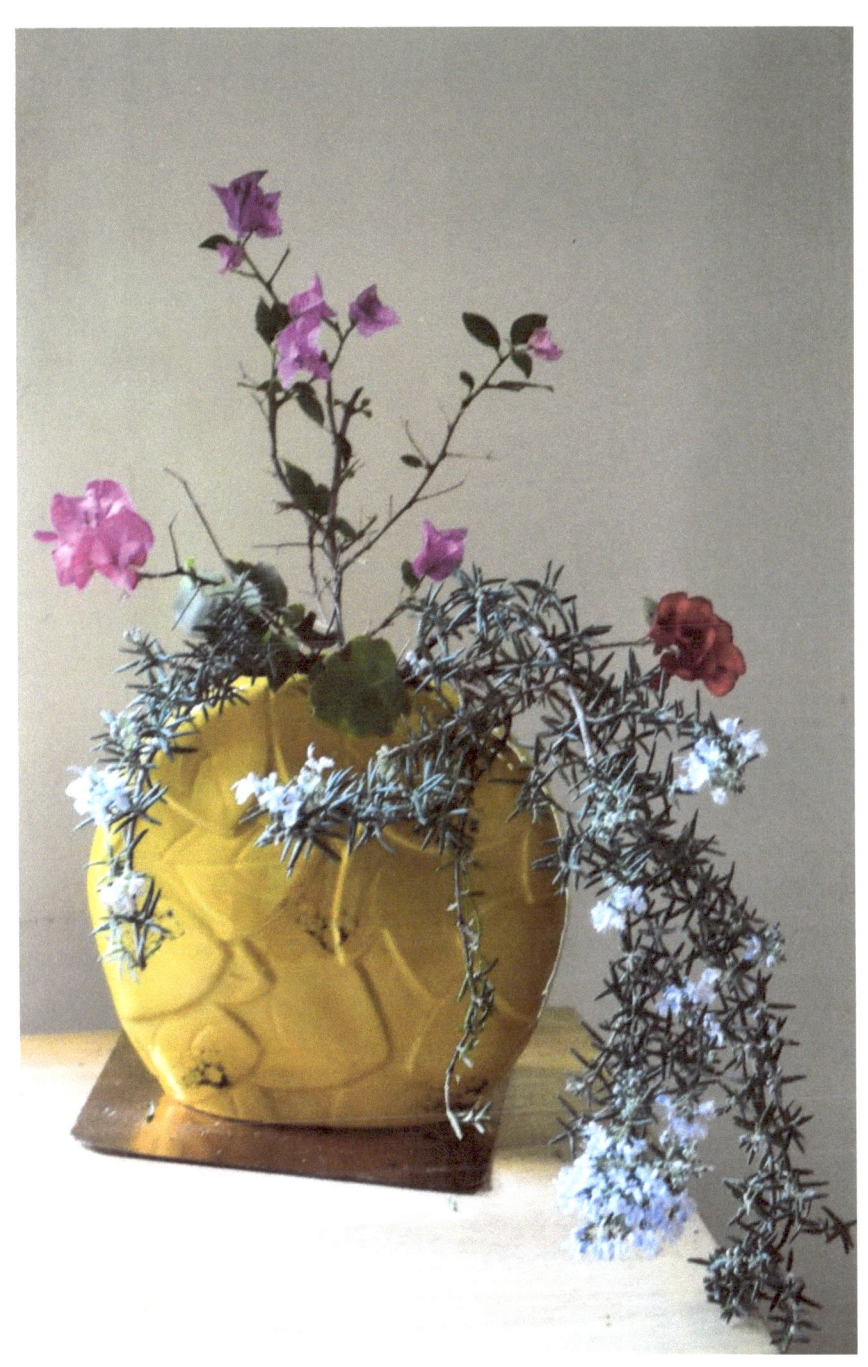

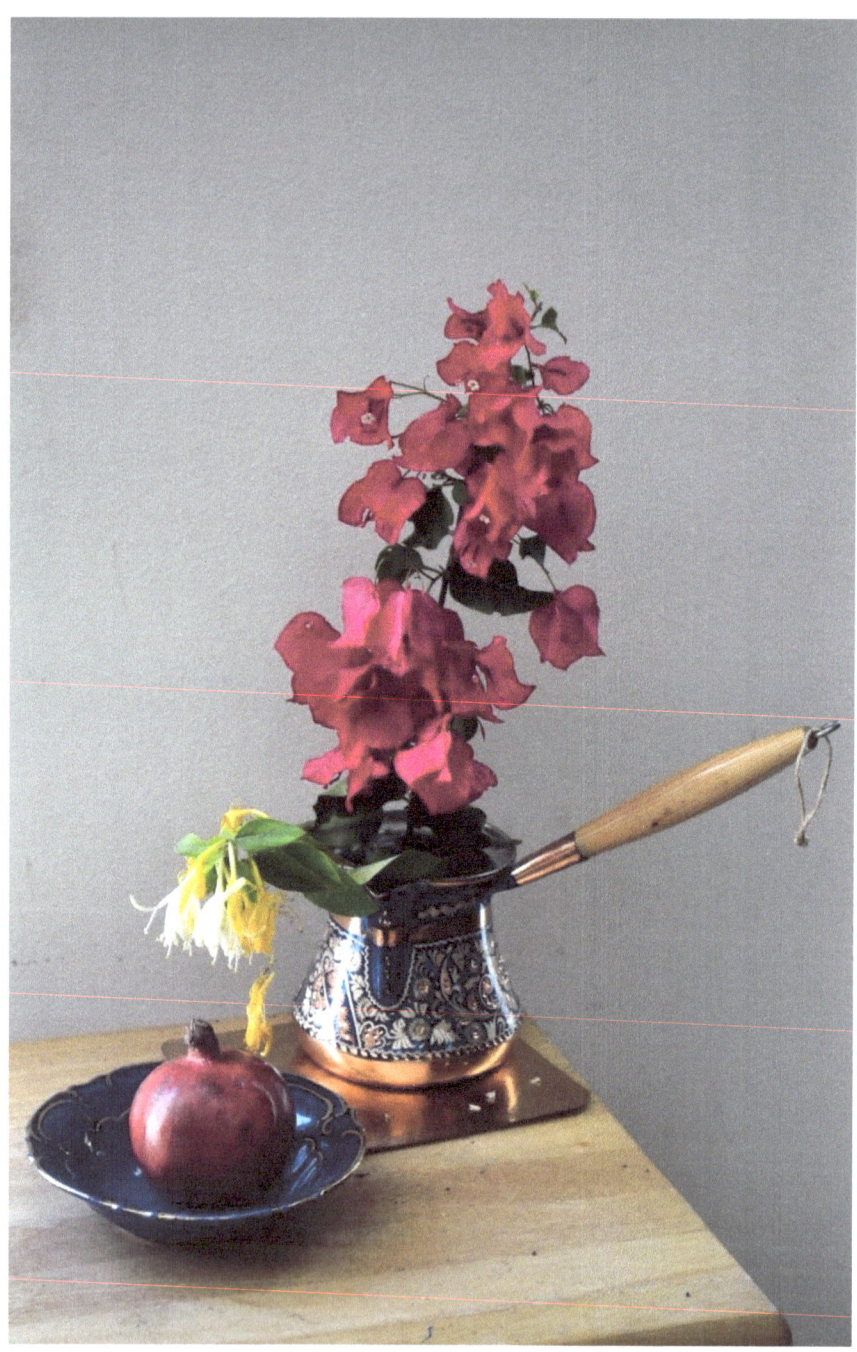

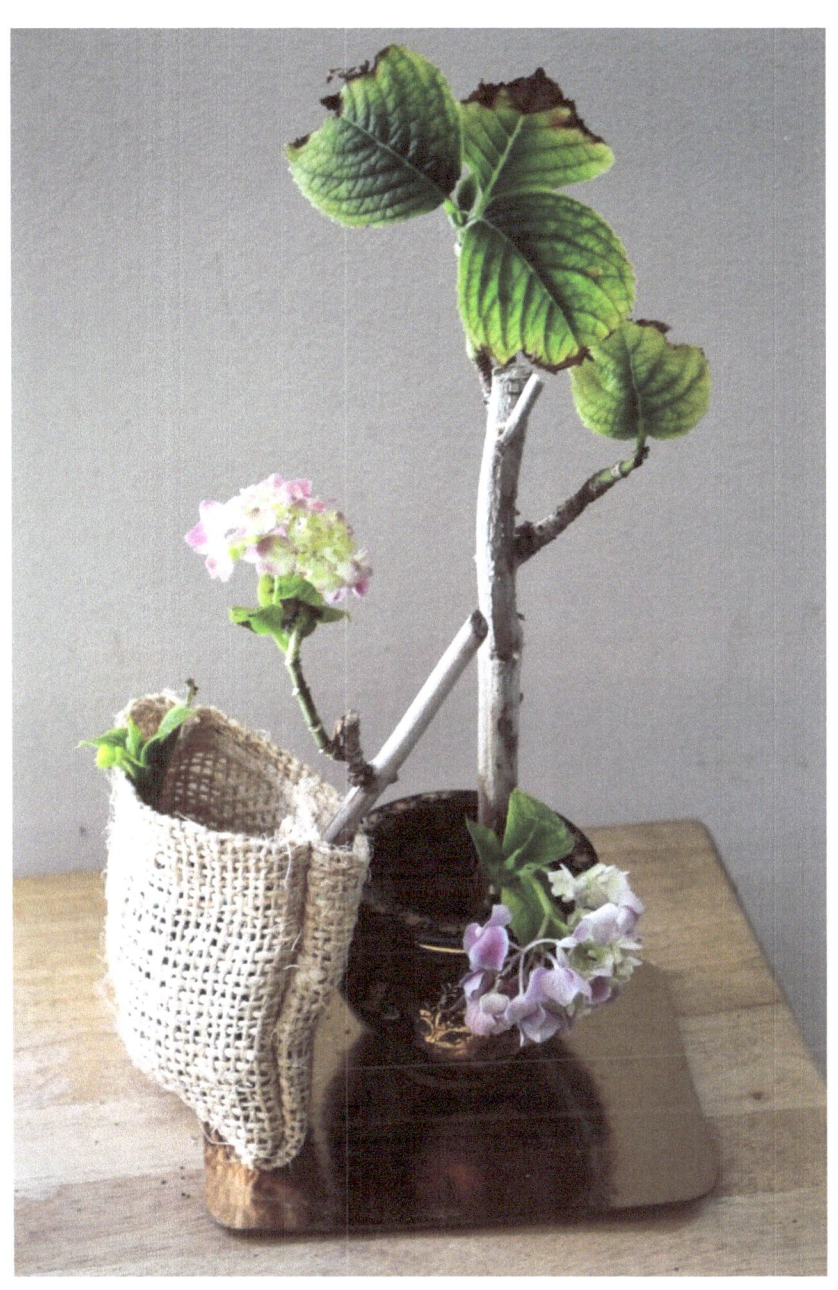

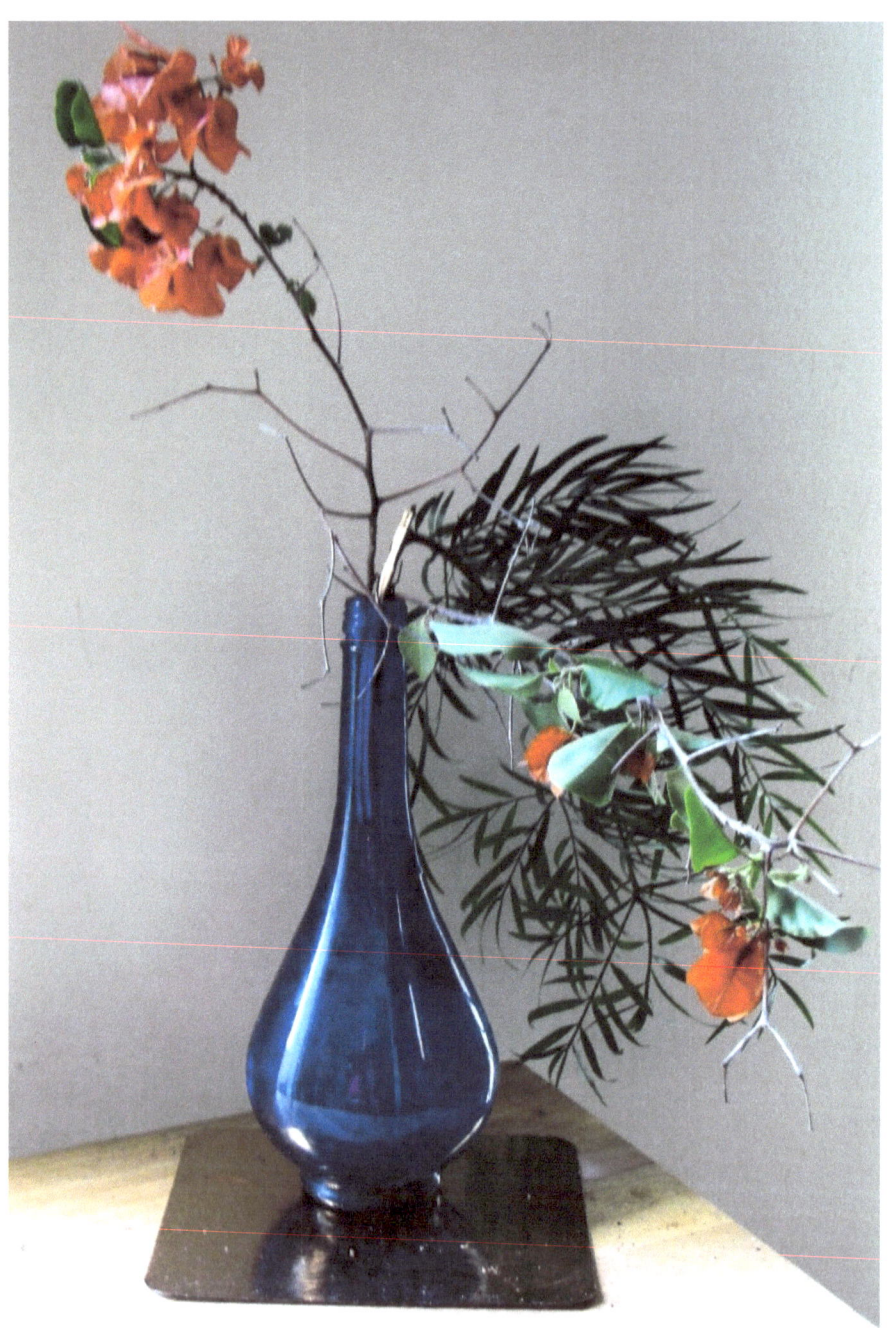

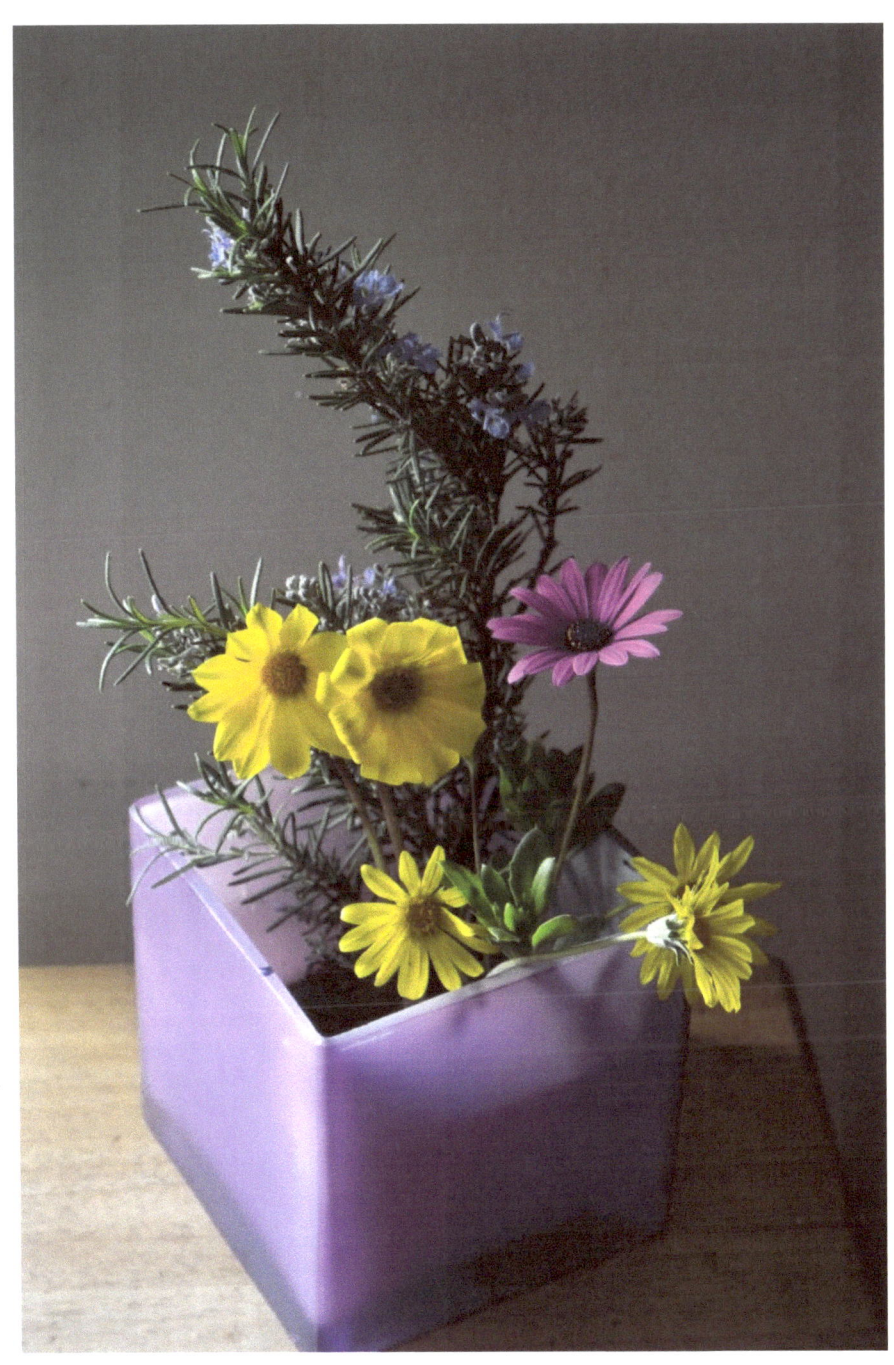

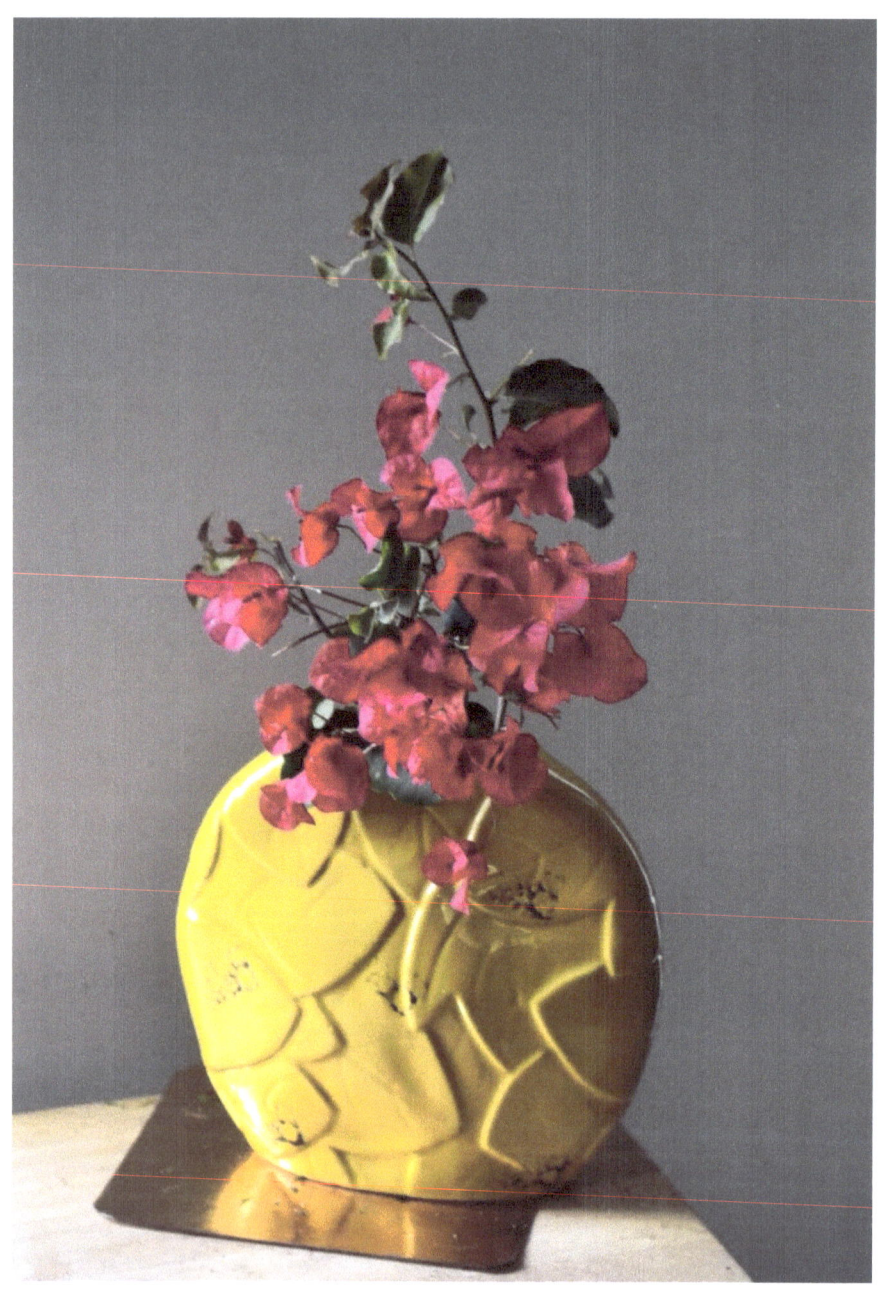

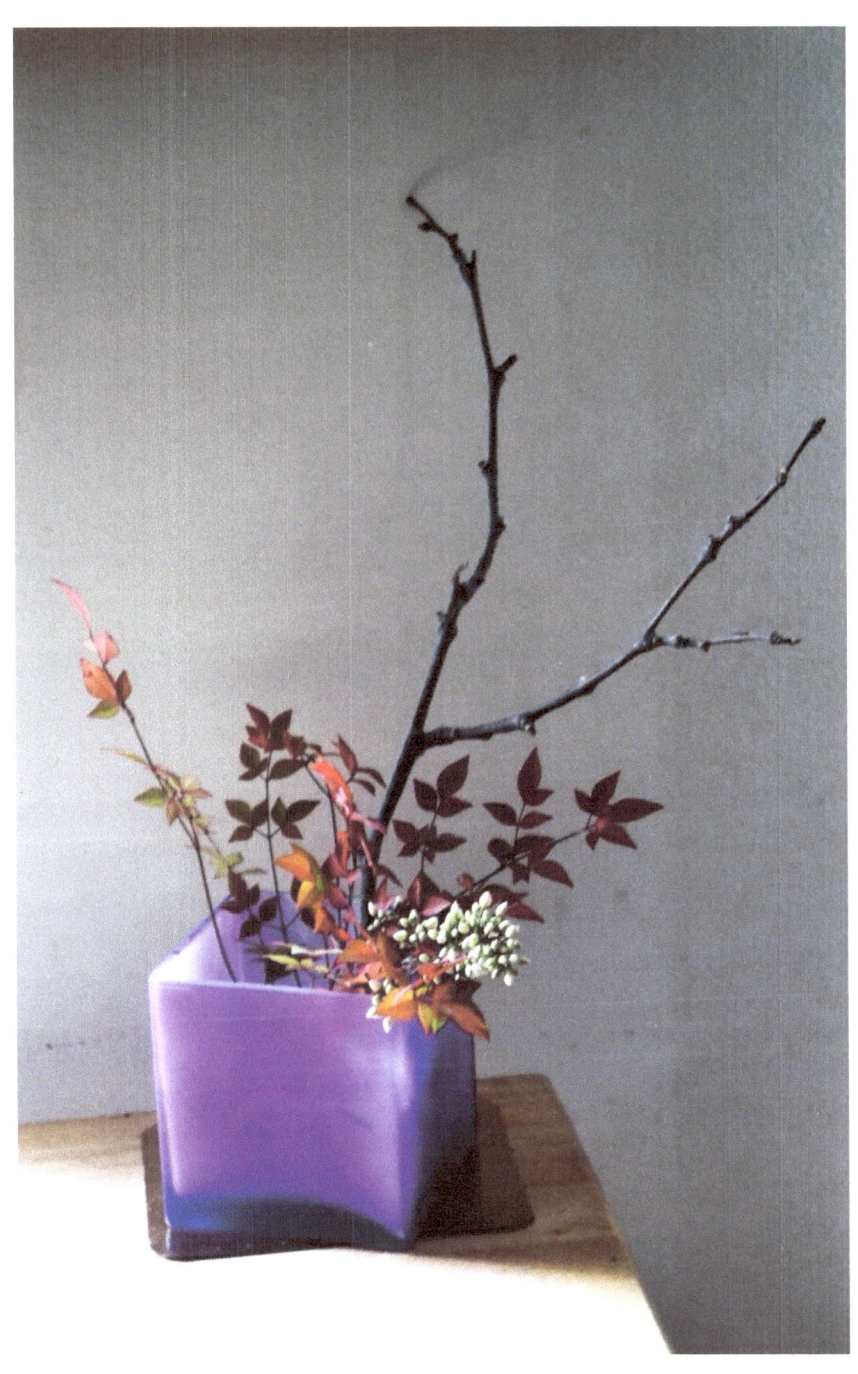

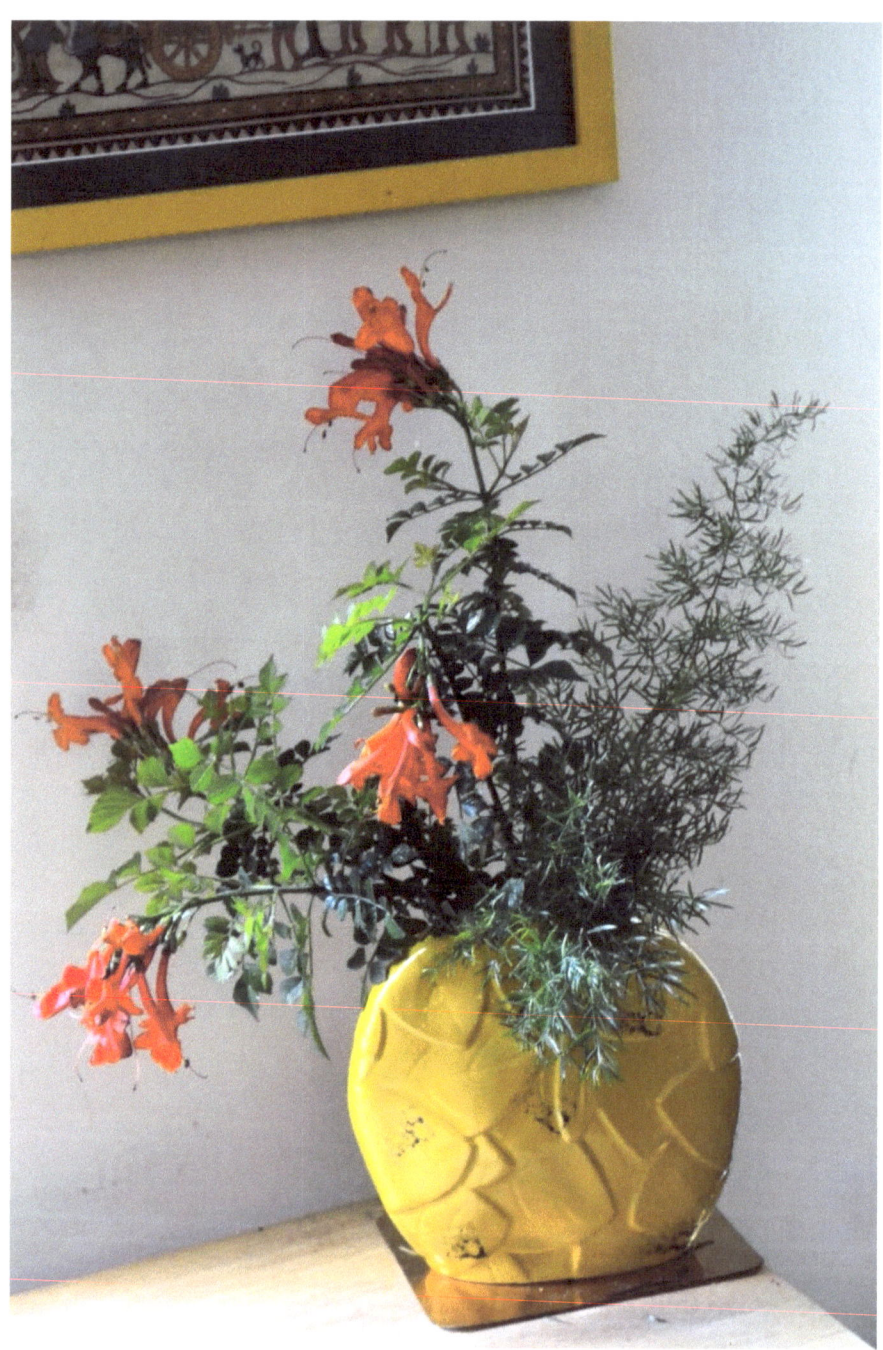

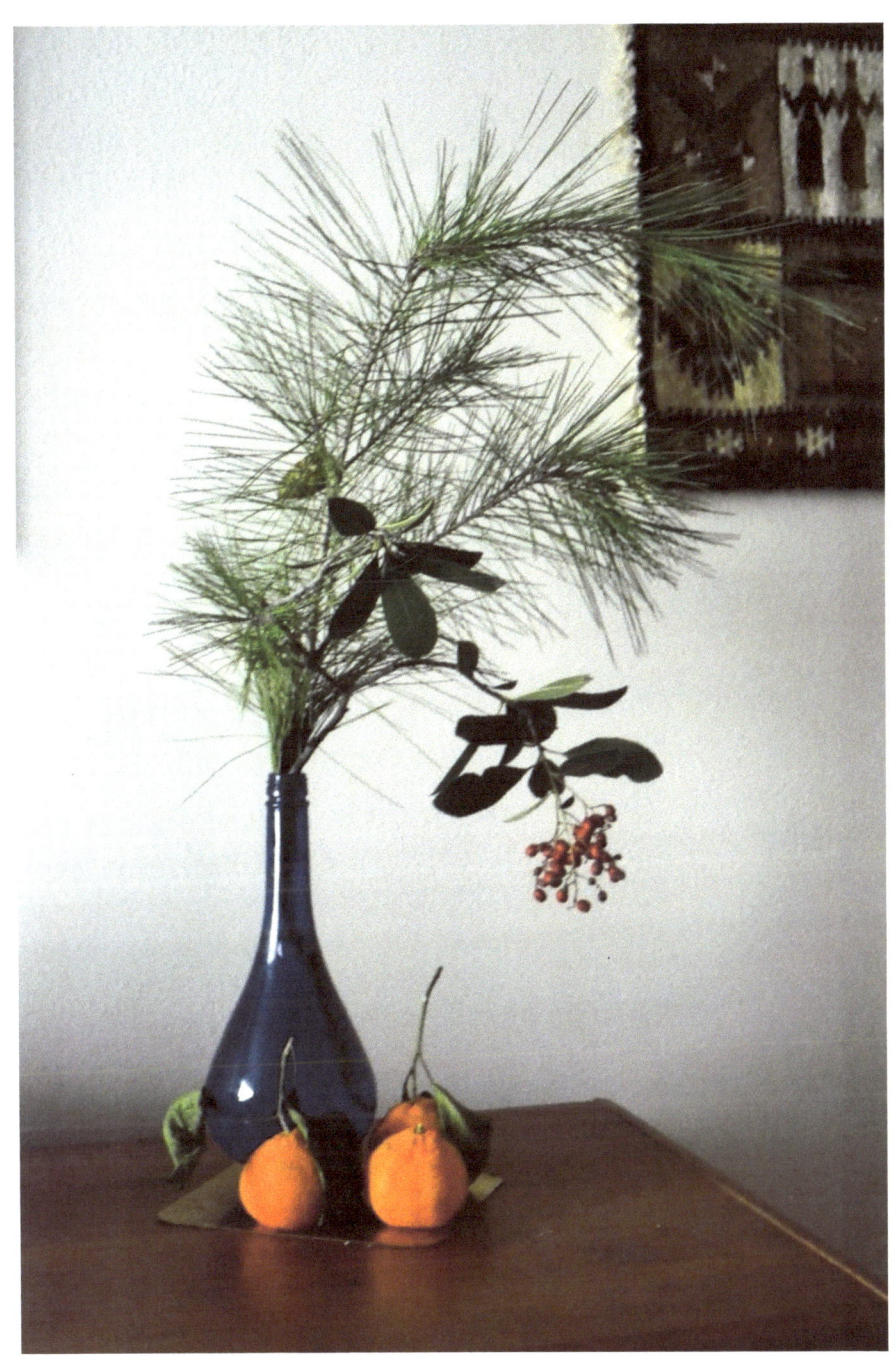

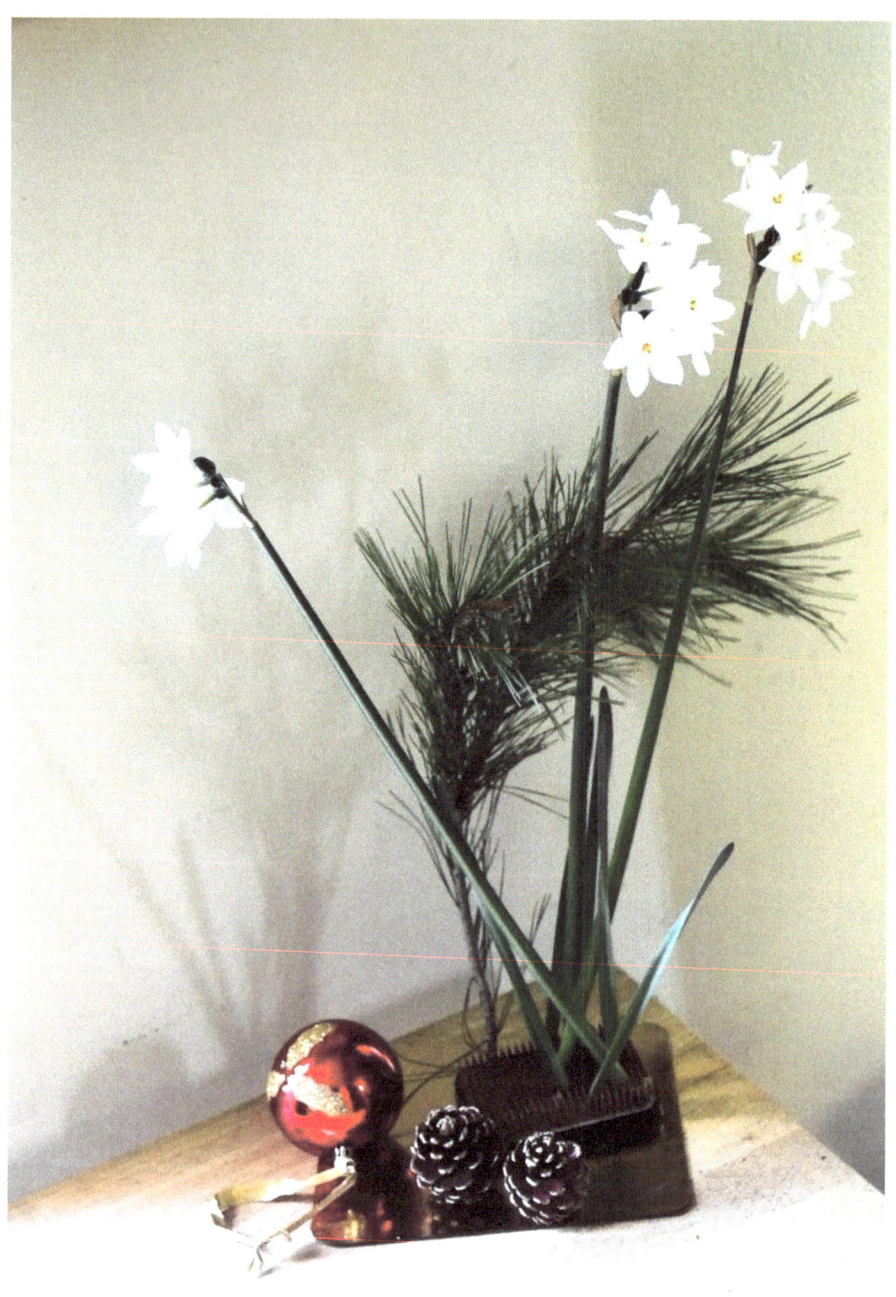

pineapple and purple statice -
a hurried ant climbing
the leafy bract

Petri dish-
a sprouting lima bean
in the sunlight

a single branch ikebana-
shadows of furry catkins
on an empty wall

alcove with hanging scroll-
fragrant honeysuckle
in reverence

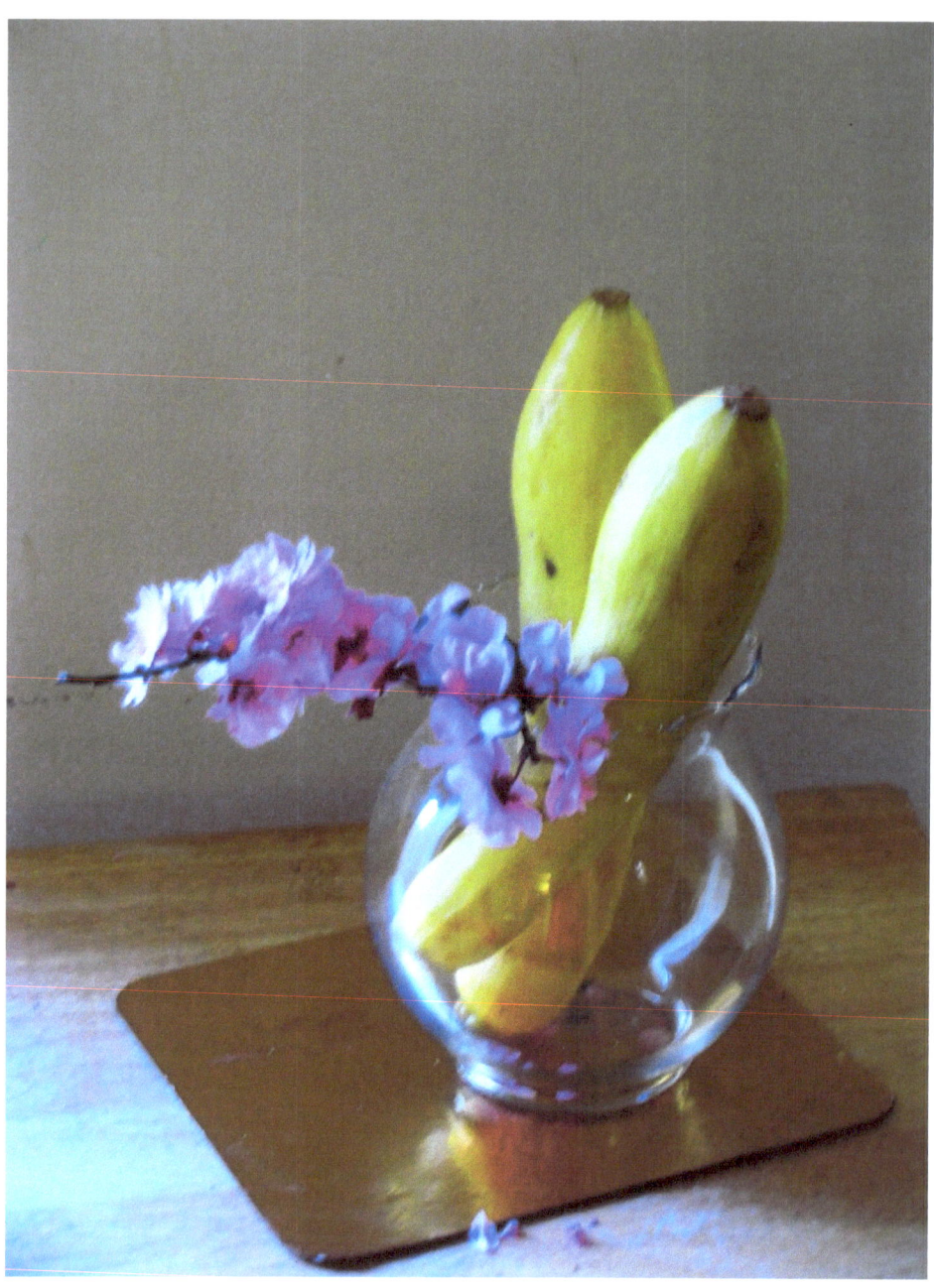

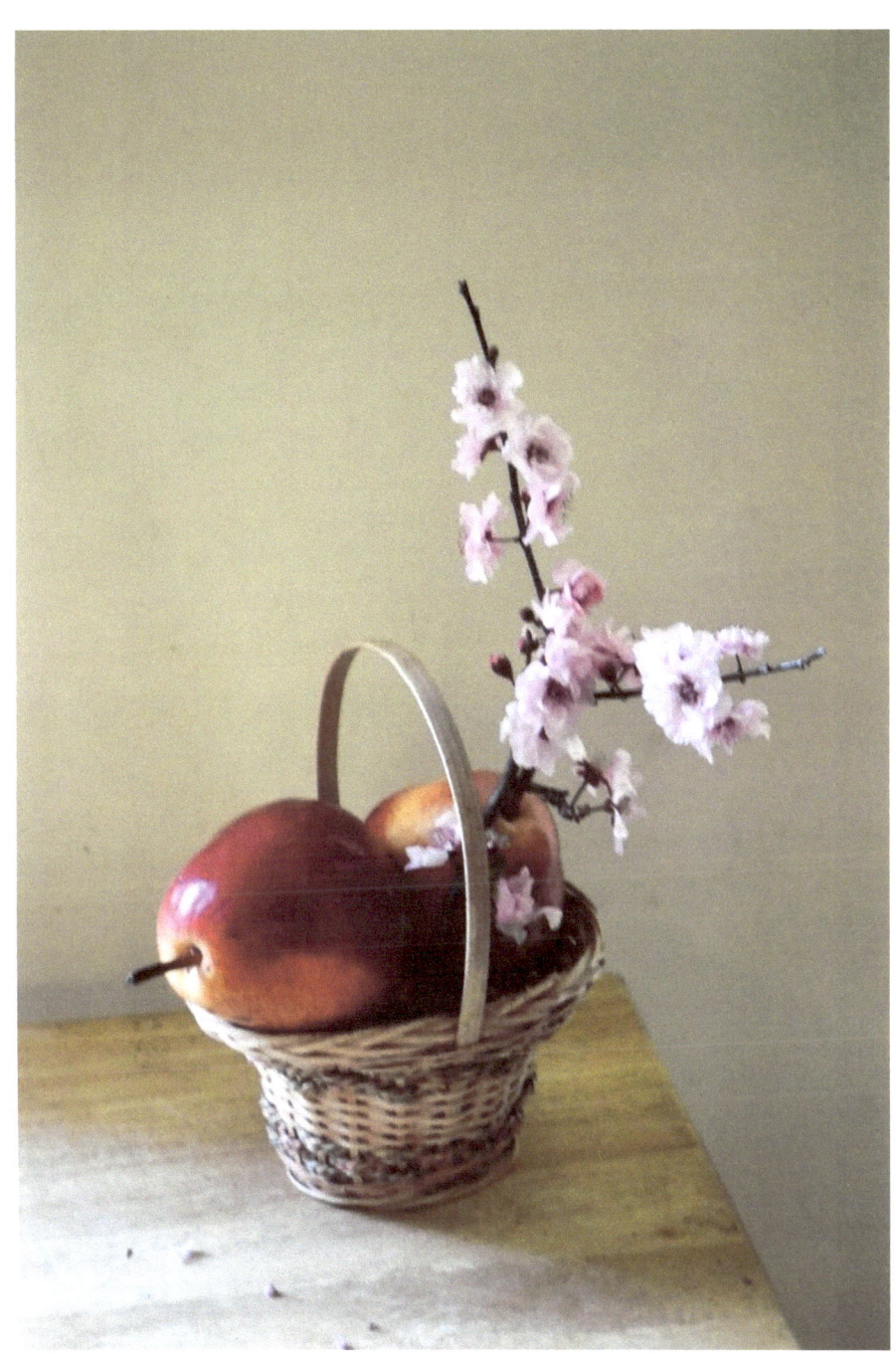

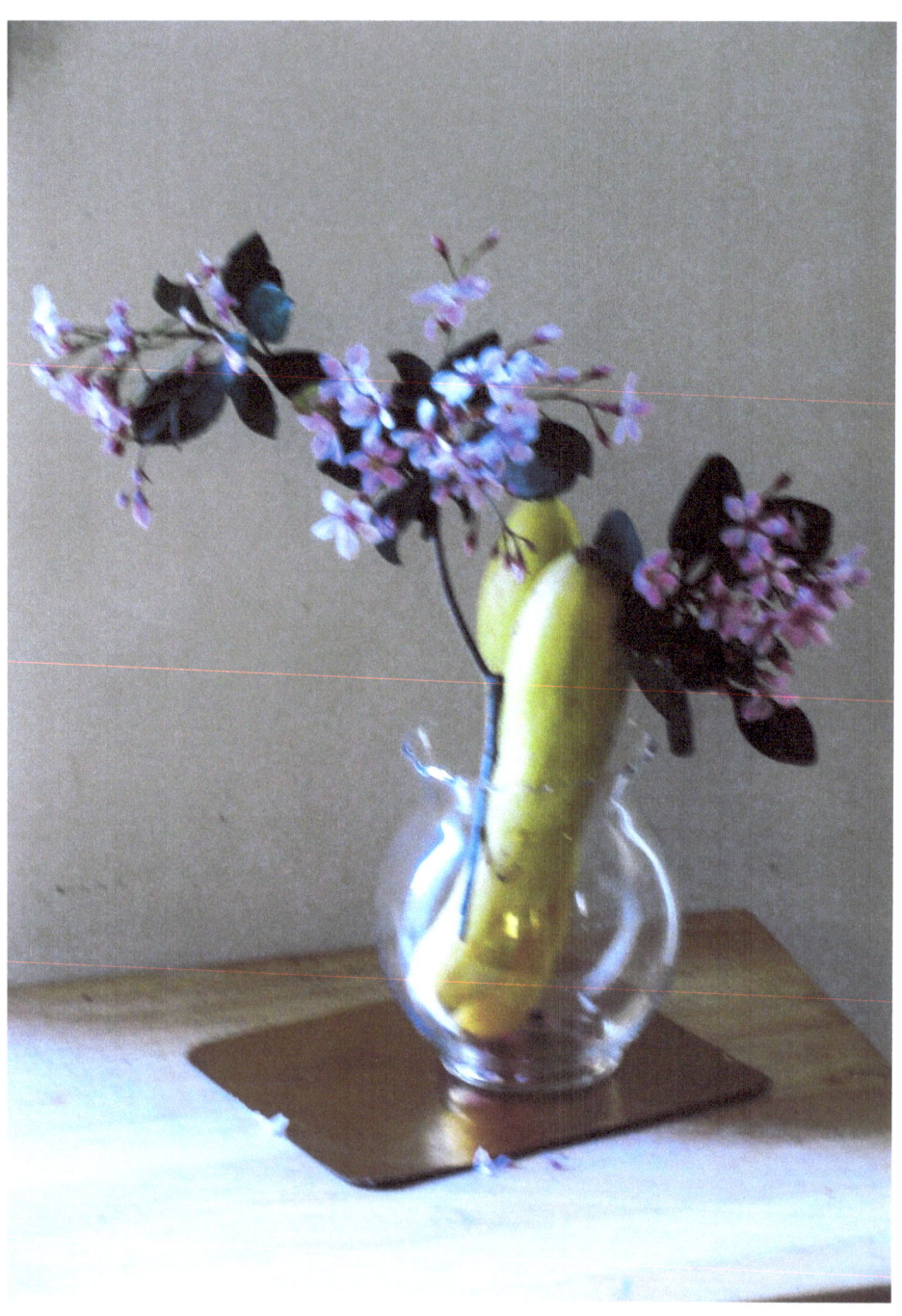

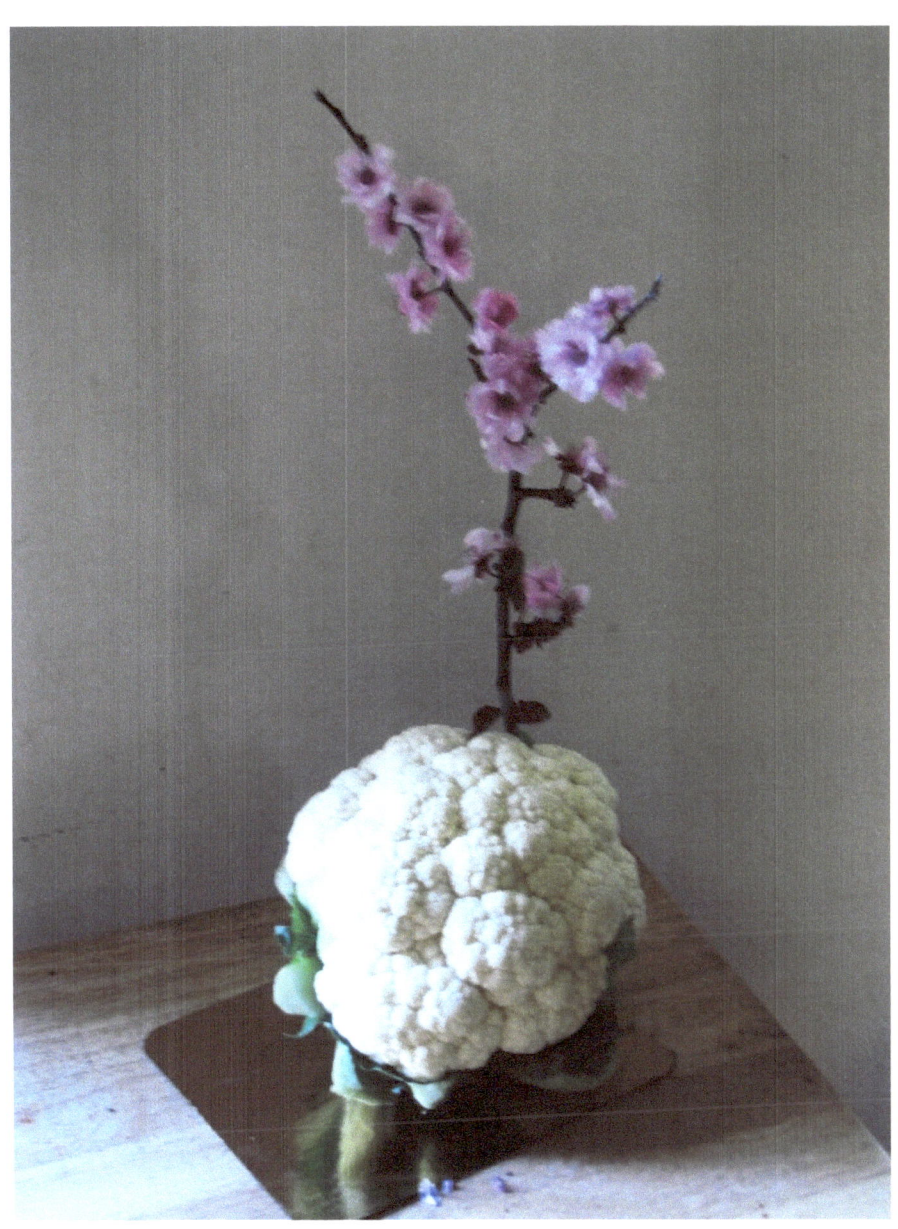

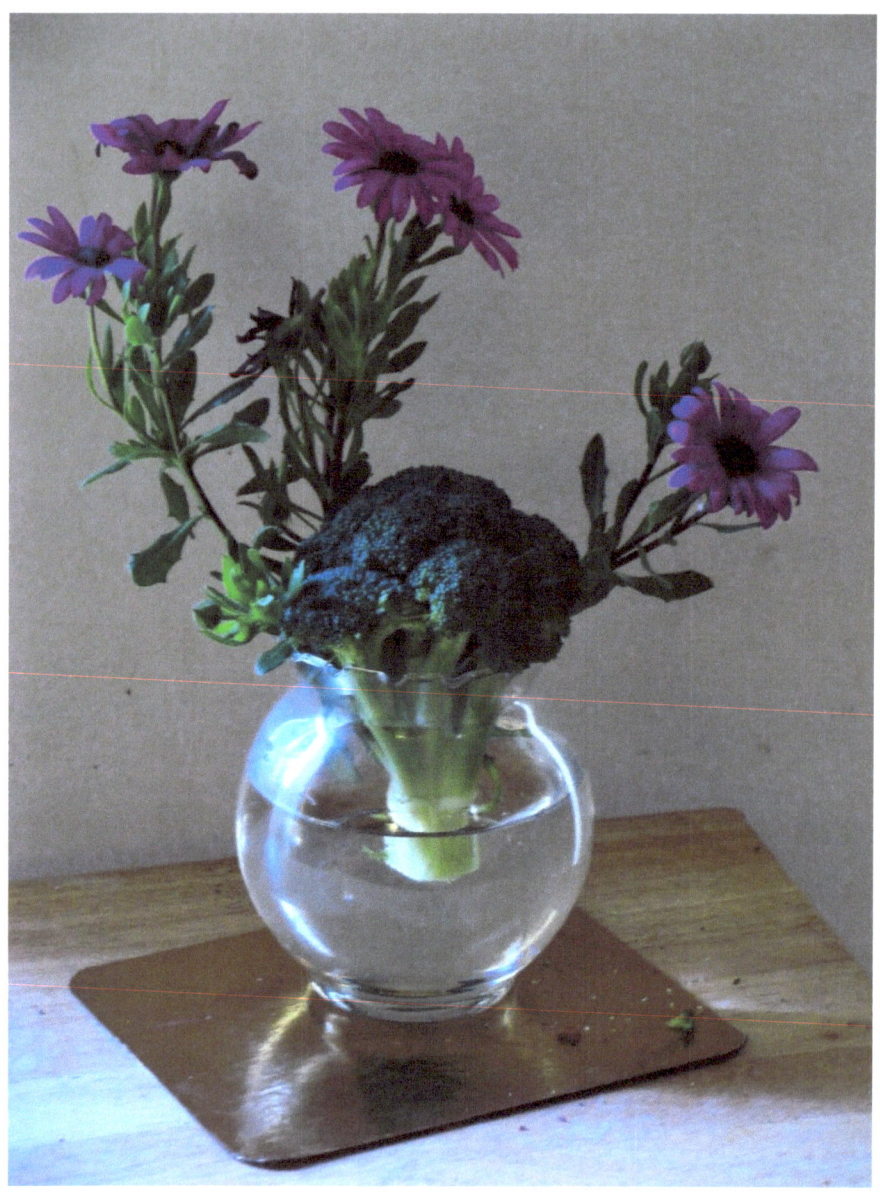

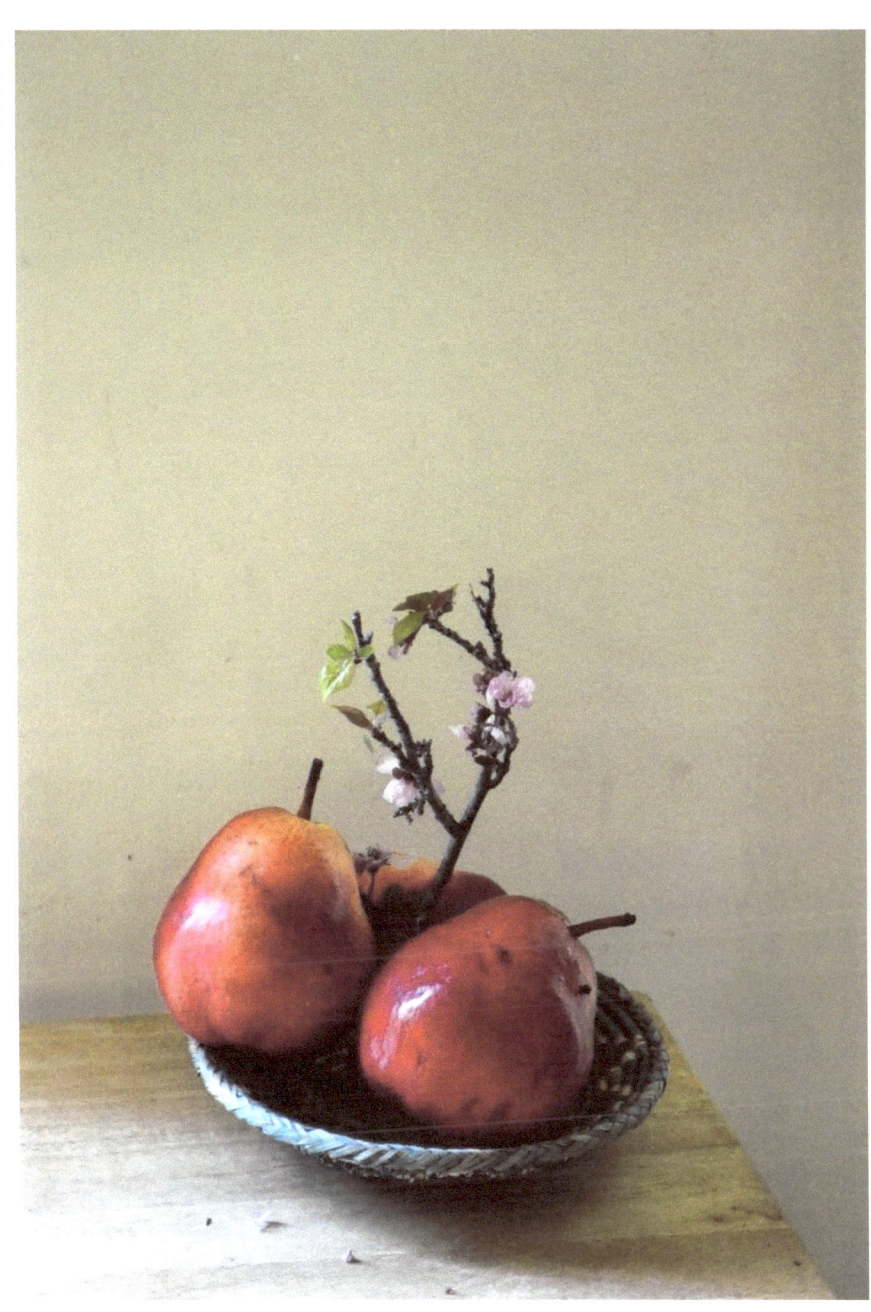

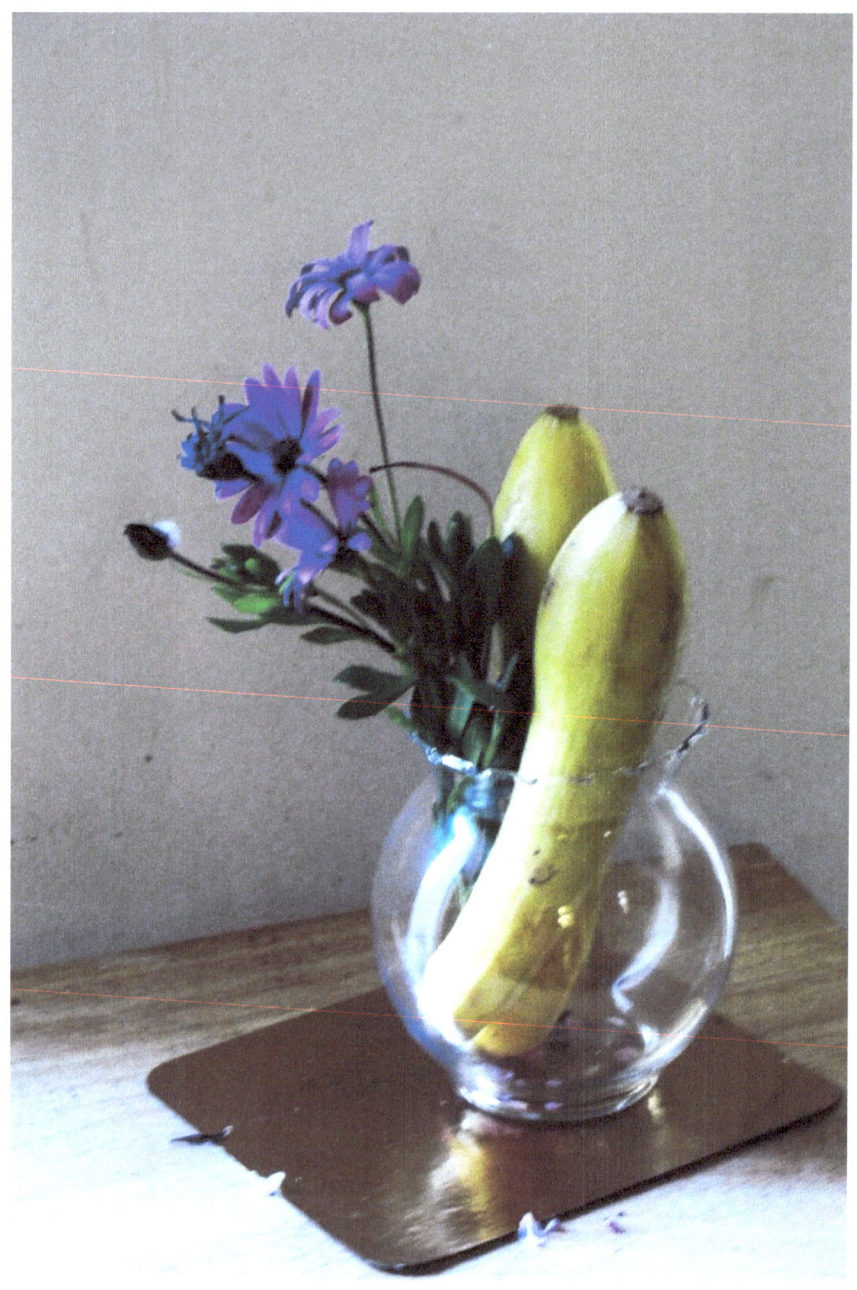

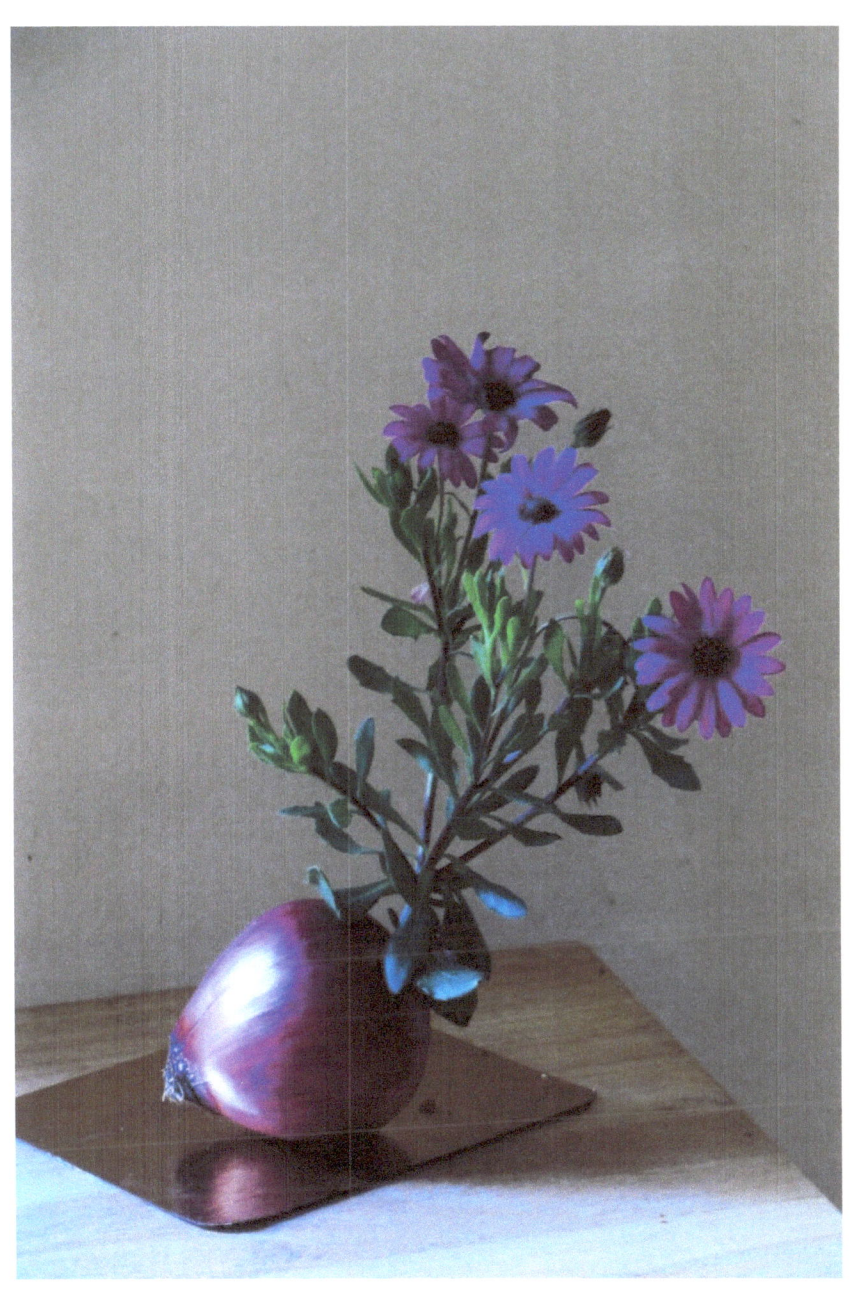

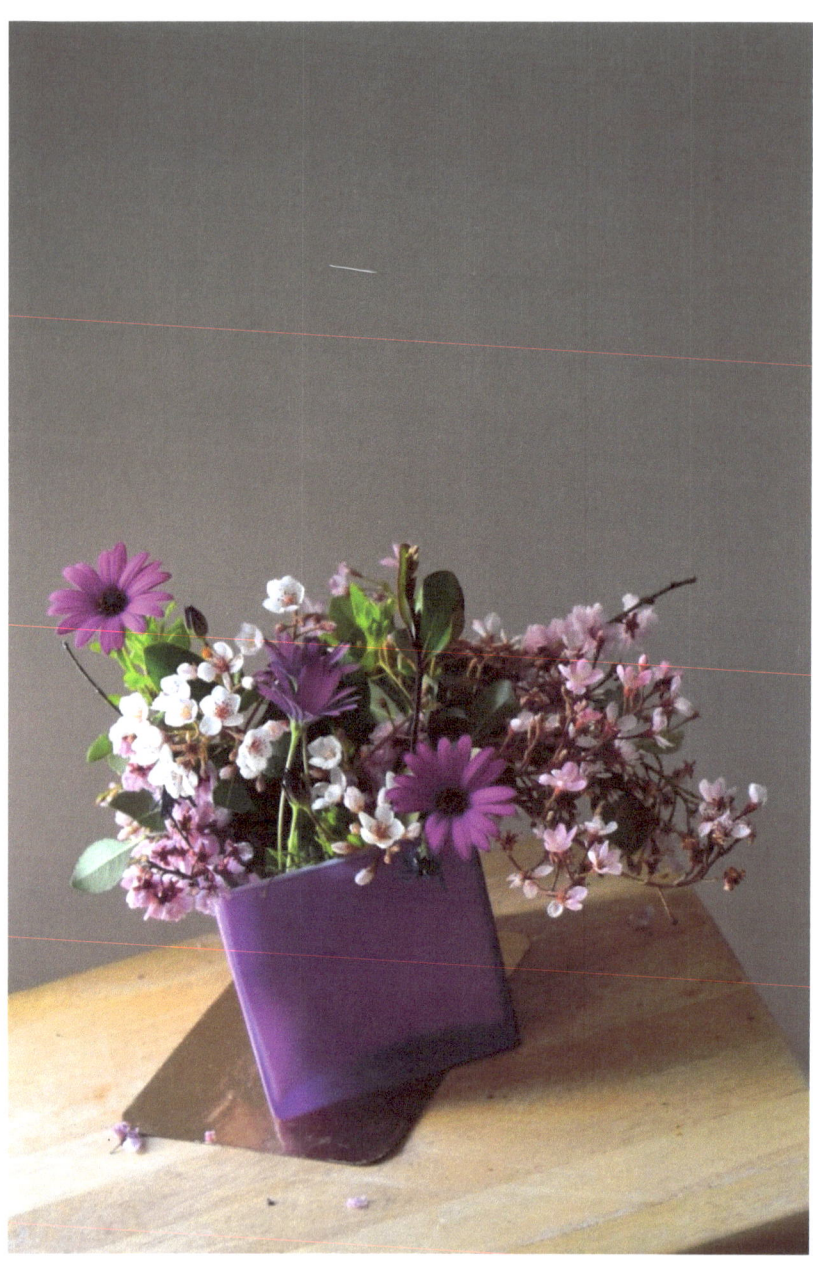

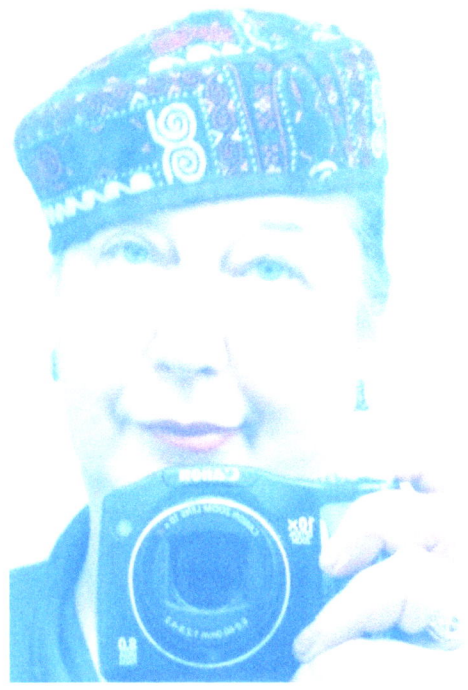

Elena Malec is a poet and fine artist with a MA in modern languages from the University of Bucharest, Romania. She has published essay and poetry in English and Romanian as well as art books for children, a fine cooking recipe book and haiku. One of her latest passions is flower arrangement following the freestyle Ikebana and Morimono art.

Her travel photos and videos, her art, and her other websites can be found at her domain:

www.emalecdesign.com